Stock Trading
A Beginner's Guide

by
Jay and Julie Hawk

First edition.

Copyright © 2017 Jay and Julie Hawk

www.thefxperts.com

All rights reserved. This book or any portion thereof
may not be reproduced or used in any manner whatsoever
without the express written permission of the authors
except for the use of brief quotations in a book review.

ISBN-13: 978-1981774845
ISBN-10: 198177484X

DEDICATION

This book is dedicated to our dear family who loved us, believed in us and encouraged us to excel in our chosen professions

JAY AND JULIE HAWK

STOCK TRADING: A BEGINNER'S GUIDE

TABLE OF CONTENTS

	Dedication	iii
	Table of Contents	v
	Acknowledgements	vii
	Foreword	ix
1	Stock Trading Basics	Pg #1
2	Getting Started Trading Stocks	Pg #25
3	About Stockbrokers	Pg #43
4	Stock Trading Strategies	Pg #55
5	Stock Price Analysis	Pg #67
6	Money Management for Stock Traders	Pg #89
7	Stock Trader Psychology	Pg #101
8	Stock Trading as a Business	Pg #117
9	Parting Advice for Stock Traders	Pg #125
10	Recommended Further Reading	Pg #129
	About the Authors	Pg #133
	Glossary	Pg #135
	Index	Pg #143

JAY AND JULIE HAWK

ACKNOWLEDGMENTS

This book is the product of many years of personal experience and research obtained by working professionally in the financial markets, trading for our own accounts, and writing about trading as freelancers. We want to thank those who brought us up, those who taught us how to trade, and those who paid us to write for them.

JAY AND JULIE HAWK

FOREWORD

As long term experts in the field of financial markets and derivatives trading, one of the most exciting things we have had the opportunity to witness personally in our careers was the electronification of the major stock markets and the advent of online trading for retail speculators. That meant individuals no longer had to be an investor or a market professional to buy and sell stocks, and they could far more efficiently trade stocks for profit.

Once that evolution happened, almost anyone could then open up a margin trading account with an online Contract for Difference or CFD broker and trade stock CFDs speculatively on margin, even if they only had a small stake to put at risk. All they needed was a reasonably modern computer connected to the Internet that they could run an electronic trading platform on. With relatively sophisticated trading software like MetaTrader 4 available freely as downloadable software, that just made the stock market even more accessible to virtually any person who wanted to get involved. This remarkable phenomenon notably changed the formerly very structured and highly regulated world of stockbroking and stock trading dramatically. Now the general public wanted to try their hands at speculating on stock price movements too!

Over the years since that major stock market evolution occurred, we have been on the forefront of educating the increasingly savvy public about how to trade stocks and other financial markets profitably. Even for many experienced traders, operating successfully in the stock market can be a challenge due to the inherent volatility of many stock prices. Inexperienced traders were further hampered by their lack of knowledge about how to trade and what fundamental factors move the stock market as a whole, as well as individual stock prices.

The harsh reality remains that without a solid foundation, most buildings do not last very long, and the same holds true for stock traders. Without a solid educational foundation and a good working understanding of how the stock market operates and how to make money consistently when trading, the margin accounts of most would-be stock operators are quickly depleted.

Knowing this all too well, we aimed to use our insider expertise obtained working as professional traders to help such retail stock traders by writing widely on the subject for numerous Internet websites so that they could freely access this insider information. Working for over a decade as freelance writers, we have at this point contributed many articles to this information pool, as well as online courses, e-books and reports. We even ghostwrote published books on the subject of financial markets that were attributed to other writers.

With this book, we offer the second in a series of planned books on the financial markets to share our knowledge and expertise in trading the stock market with the public in a different format. Our intention in publishing a book under our own names is to take a higher-profile role in educating prospective traders realistically about what is involved in trading stocks profitably and to complement the background of more experienced traders with professional methods and techniques that they may not yet be familiar with. Successful stock trading is not exactly easy, but it does not have to be overly difficult either, especially with access to the proper tools and education.

This beginner's guide to stock trading is designed to give traders and prospective traders a solid foundation to build upon as they operate in the stock market. We intend to do this by sharing our insider knowledge about the different established trading methods and market analysis tools. We also share what worked for us as we took the benefit of our differing professional backgrounds and applied our knowledge to the task of trading stock CFDs in our own personal accounts using MetaTrader4 and the easy stock market access offered by online CFD brokers.

In addition to covering the basics about the equity markets that any stock trader needs to know, this book contains detailed information about opening an online trading account and getting familiar with using an electronic trading platform. It also covers how to get started trading stocks using some basic trading strategies and money management techniques that can be applied immediately in your trading business.

The chapter on stock price analysis introduces the trader to the essential tools of technical analysis as it pertains to stocks, which can be extremely useful in determining entry and exit points for trades. We also introduce the other major analysis method of fundamental analysis, since such factors can often move the market regardless of a stock's technical condition and need to be a part of any trader's understanding of the equity market.

Further on the book, our chapter on money management explains optimal ways of managing risk for the size of your trading account and gives the trader prudent position sizing and other money management techniques to start applying immediately. What many novice traders fail to realize is that by using an intelligent method of money management, a stock trader can be successful even if they are wrong more than half of the time on the direction of the market.

We think that one of the most important segments of this book is the trader psychology chapter since understanding your psychological makeup and how to manage your emotions when trading is a key element to success. Knowing how you react to different market situations and cultivating the optimal trading mindset can really make the difference between turning a profit or a loss in the stock market. This section of the book illustrates the various types of traders and explains how they typically react to different market situations and emotional experiences.

In the next chapter of this book, we put together the knowledge from previous chapters to help the reader make stock trading a viable business proposition for them and any potential investors they might wish to attract. Our chapter on stock trading as a business distills the methods previously illustrated to help you run a successful stock trading business, just as we have run our trading business. Using appropriate discretion, a comprehensive and easy to follow trading plan, and sound money management techniques, we think that any person of reasonable intelligence can become a successful stock trader.

We then conclude the book by offering some helpful tips that we learned when we started to trade that contributed to our success, and that we think any trader would probably benefit from internalizing. We also provide a glossary of terms you can refer to as you start to decipher the often colorful jargon that professional stock traders use to communicate with each other; some recommended additional reading to further your trading education; and a bit of information about our professional backgrounds to establish our authority to educate on this subject.

While the age-old trading goal of "buying low and selling high" continues to be the key when pursuing a profit in any market, having some decent insider knowledge under your belt can help you better discern what levels are high and what levels are low. This does not mean that traders need to overcomplicate their trading decisions; especially since many of the most successful stock trading plans and techniques can be extremely simple and are often the most profitable since they are the easiest to apply quickly in a fast moving market.

Overall, we think this second book on trading in our financial series makes an excellent introduction to what can appear to be a complicated subject. In writing it, we intended for this introductory book to inspire and educate both novice and seasoned traders alike, and we wish our readers great success in their stock trading careers and hope they enjoy them as much as we have ours.

Jay and Julie Hawk
www.thefxperts.com
Sonora, Mexico, December, 2017

CHAPTER 1: STOCK TRADING BASICS

What is a stock exactly? Well, a stock represents an interest or share in a company's ownership. Stock, or equity as it is sometimes called, represents a claim by the owner on the issuing company's earnings and assets. A single share of stock represents a partial ownership of the issuing company in proportion to the total outstanding shares, and acquiring more stock in a company means your ownership stake becomes larger.

Furthermore, any introduction to stock trading needs to clarify that a stock, share or equity purchase transaction involves the exchange of currency for a certificate of stock, while a stock sale transaction involves the exchange of a stock certificate for currency. The price at which this transaction or trade takes place is determined by market factors such as the supply and demand for the stock.

Stocks typically trade on exchanges or organized marketplaces where transactions are subject to local regulations. Many of these stock exchanges exist in countries around the world listing the stock of local corporations, and cross-border stock investment transactions are also possible in many jurisdictions. As of 2016, the various local stock markets around the world experienced a total yearly transaction volume of just over 77.5 trillion U.S. Dollars, according to data provided by the World Bank citing the database maintained by the World Federation of Exchanges.

A Second Income from Trading Stocks?

Fortunately, the ability to execute stock transactions has never been as readily available to so many people, as it is today. Gone are the days when a normal person had to call their stockbroker to find out where the market was trading on a particular company's shares or check the stock closing price listings in a major newspaper.

The 21st century has truly arrived with respect to the various stock markets, as modern technology and the rise of Contract for Difference or CFD trading makes them accessible to a wide online audience that grows daily. Thanks to this new opportunity to trade stocks online, many people can also work jobs as they trade equities in their spare time. Some of the more successful traders have even used their income trading stocks to replace their jobs so they can now enjoy more time at home with their families.

If taking the risks inherent in trading stocks seems right for your particular financial situation, do remember to cultivate the discipline and patience that will keep you in business as a stock trader over the long term. Reading this book thoroughly will definitely set you on the right track to success as a stock trader, but having the discipline typically required to trade profitably is entirely up to you.

A Brief History of Stock Markets

Stock trading has its roots back in 12th century France, where debt regulators working on behalf of banks operated in rural agricultural communities. In 1460, the first centralized exchange opened in Antwerp, Belgium.

Nevertheless, the stock exchange considered the first in the world was the Amsterdam Stock Exchange. This exchange was established in 1602 by the Dutch East India Company or Verenigde Oostindische Compagnie, which was also the first company to issue stocks and bonds.

Stock exchanges began popping up in Spain and Portugal to manage the enormous wealth these nations were plundering from the Americas. With the expansion of the British Empire and the end of the Napoleonic wars, Britain became the new center for world commerce during the late 18th and 19th centuries.

Stock Trading Takes Hold in the Colonies

The newly formed United States had a great need for developing economically. The first U.S. Secretary of the Treasury, Alexander Hamilton, had studied the British exchanges and believed that stock exchanges were a key element in developing and maintaining a healthy economy.

While Hamilton was subsequently in office as U.S. president between 1789 and 1795, he encouraged the trading of government debt securities on the corner of Wall and Broad Streets under a buttonwood tree in New York City. At the time, New York was the U.S. capitol.

By 1817, trading on that corner had become quite hectic, with a large number of participants buying and selling not only government securities, but also stocks. The traders united at this point to charge outsiders a small commission on trades which became known as the Buttonwood Agreement.

The newly organized traders then moved into the building at 40 Wall Street, and the New York Stock and Exchange Board was founded in 1817. This was later to become known as the New York Stock Exchange. A competing organization located just down the street called the New York Curb Exchange also went indoors in the year 1842. It later changed its name to the American Stock Exchange.

The Boom of the 1920's

During the early part of the 20th century, the stock exchanges generally flourished, seeing increasing trade in both stocks and bonds. Trading became extremely speculative after the First World War, with people trading stocks on as little as 10% margin.

Trading stocks had become universal, as all kinds of people began investing and speculating on stock price moves. By 1929, the U.S. stock market had soared to new heights, and by September 3rd of that year, the Dow Jones Industrial Average had reached a peak of 381.17.

Black Tuesday

Nevertheless, U.S. stock prices started sliding from that buoyant level, and on Monday, October 28th, the market make a record fall of almost 13%, ending at 260.64. The following day of October 29th is now known as Black Tuesday, and it saw the market crash further on a record trading volume of 16 million shares to lose over 11% of its value and close at 230.07.

The U.S. stock market subsequently declined over the next three years, leaving the DJIA at a low of 41.22 on July 8th 1932. By 1934, the government stepped in and introduced the Securities and Exchange Act and the Securities and Exchange Commission or SEC which has regulated trading in stocks ever since.

Other Stock Market Crashes

Other notable stock market crashes occurred in the years 1973-74, on Black Monday in 1987, after the Dot Com bubble burst in 2000, and during the most recent financial crisis in 2008. The most notable of these was the Crash of 1987, which affected stock markets worldwide.

The October 19th 1987 crash saw prices decline 22.6% on the DJIA that day alone, as shown in Figure 1 below, and the precipitous drop quickly spread to exchanges all over the world. By the end of the month, Hong Kong stocks had lost 45.8%, U.K. stocks had lost 26%, Australian stocks were down 42%, and the Canadian stock market had fallen 22.5%.

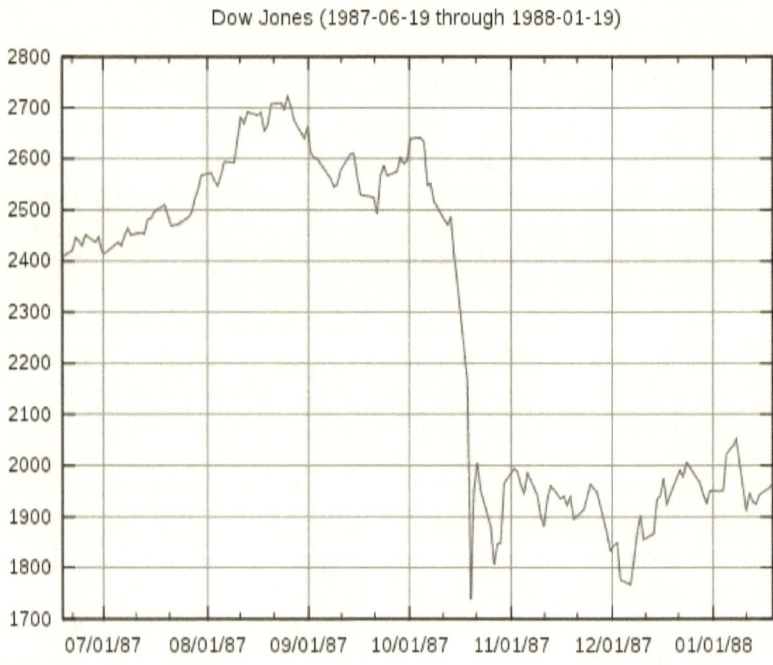

Figure 1: A chart of the Dow Jones Industrial Average around the time of the Black Monday stock market crash in 1987.

Since then, stock exchanges have adopted "circuit breakers" which means that after a certain percentage decline, 10% for the NYSE for example, trading is halted for a period, and then trading resumes. These circuit breakers are still in effect today.

Different Types of Stocks

The stock market has traditionally been the center for transactions involving buying and selling different corporate securities. Several types of stocks can be found trading both on exchanges and on Electronic Communications Networks or ECN's.

This section gives a general overview of the different types of stocks that traders and investors typically trade. Traders typically classify stocks into the two primary groups described below, which are common and preferred stock, and some also include securities that are convertible into stock.

Common Stock

When most people refer to stock, common stock is generally what they are talking about. Common stock consists of a form of security issued by a corporation which represents the most basic division of ownership in that company.

Common stock usually has voting rights. This means that when the company is involved in major decisions, such as selecting a Chief Executive Officer or the Board of Directors or expanding the company by issuing new shares for example, the stockholders are entitled to vote on these matters.

The holder of common stock also participates in the earnings of the company in the form of dividend payments. Nevertheless, many corporations do not pay dividends on their common stock these days.

Preferred Stock

Preferred stock refers to stock which has an advantage over common shares in that it gets preferential treatment in the case of the liquidation of the corporation due to situations like bankruptcy, for example. While a safer investment, such stock is not as heavily-traded or as popular as common stock, and it has other notable differences as well.

For example, many corporation pay out regular dividends on their preferred stock, while they may forgo paying a dividend completely on their common stock. Nevertheless, depending on the company involved, the preferred stock in most cases does not have voting rights or has limited voting rights.

Another significant difference arises from the fact that a company's preferred stock will generally sell at a premium to its common stock, often because of the increased safety and return of the security. Furthermore, preferred stock may not enjoy as liquid a market as the corporation's common stock since most companies issue less preferred stock.

Interestingly, many preferred stocks are "callable" which means that the corporation may purchase back or redeem these shares at their option at any time at a certain price. Of course, a company calling preferred stock generally involves buying back the shares at or above the current trading price.

Also, many preferred stocks come in several classes in order to restrict voting rights to one group of investors over another. These stocks usually have labels such as "preferred A stock" or "preferred B stock", and they can differ both with respect to price and their place within the company's liquidation of assets hierarchy.

Convertible Securities

Besides common and preferred stocks, companies sometimes offer convertible securities to investors. Convertible securities can take the form of either bonds which are convertible into stock or preferred stock that can subsequently be changed into a higher number of shares of common stock by the investor on specified terms.

Convertible preferred stocks are shares of preferred stock which have a convertibility option for the shareholder. Convertible preferred stocks will usually have a time requirement for holding them before the shares can be converted.

When exercised at any time after a certain specified date, their convertibility option entitles the holder to convert the preferred shares into common stock at the conversion ratio specified in its prospectus. Convertible preferred shares are also known as "convertible preference shares" in the United Kingdom.

Also, stocks that are convertible and/or preferred have unique rights and specifications which you should investigate before purchasing by reading their prospectus carefully.

Furthermore, purchasing types of stock other than common stock seems more widespread among investors than among speculating stock traders due to the greater liquidity and resulting tighter bid/offer spreads usually seen in the market for common stocks.

Basically, it pays to be well-informed about what securities you are trading and to be clear about whether you wish to trade stocks in order to invest or to speculate.

Trading Stocks

In order to trade stocks, getting some basic knowledge about stocks trading before putting money at risk can be extremely beneficial to the novice.

Knowing the nature of stocks and their role in the world of investing and finance can be invaluable to anyone considering investing in the stock market. This section discusses several key aspects of stock trading that people should know in order to trade stocks.

The Stock Market and Why Stocks are Important

Basically, a stock represents an ownership right to a corporation. This contrasts to a bond which is a debt instrument issued to a creditor of a corporation. Furthermore, stock owners are subordinate to bond owners in the priority of a corporation's financing.

Why do companies issue stock? Companies issue and trade stocks for a variety of reasons. One of the main reasons has to do with spreading the risk of ownership, and another important motivation involves financing the expansion of the corporation.

Example of a Corporation Issuing Stock

When corporations are formed, the government requires that they have a corporate charter. In it, the corporation needs to state the intentions of the corporation and how much stock in the corporation exists. The charter also names the main stockholders of the corporation, who would consist of the initial owners of the corporation.

The corporation's charter will typically carry provisions for the issuing of stock to the public if the company decides to become a publicly-traded company. Otherwise, the company can remain private with the shares of the company's stock remaining in private hands. The stock of the corporation can also be offered to outside parties through a private transaction.

Stocks trading in this manner are typically transacted between parties privately without the need of a centralized exchange. Basically, the company remains private and the transaction occurs between the corporation and an individual investor, for example.

Issuing Stock to the Public

When a corporation decides it needs a large influx of capital to expand operations, or has determined that spreading the risk of the original investment was in the best interests of the original stockholders, the corporation can choose to take the company public.

Most corporations include clauses in their charter for this eventuality, with a pre-determined amount of stock set aside for issuance in the event of an Initial Public Offering or IPO. When the time for an IPO comes, the corporation will require the services of an investment banker to determine a fair price and to distribute the newly-issued stock to the public.

The corporation may also issue more than one type of stock, such as "preferred stock." In addition, stocks trading often begins privately before the new stocks are offered to the general public.

Listed and Unlisted Stocks

Listed stocks refer to stocks trading on a centralized stock exchange such as the New York Stock Exchange or NYSE. Unlisted stocks are not listed on an exchange and generally trade over a network. The latter are considered "Over-The-Counter" or OTC stocks.

Interestingly, OTC stocks include some big corporate names like Microsoft and Sun Microsystems. Both of these corporations have preferred to continue trading on the OTC market, despite the prestige associated with NYSE-traded companies.

While stocks trading OTC offer investors the advantage of not paying exchange fees, the lack of a centralized trading location can make for increased volatility.

Basically, trading in commodities or currencies in most cases involves pure speculation on price or exchange-rate fluctuations. On the other hand, those who trade stocks will often be making a longer-term investment in a company's future.

Investing in Stocks

While stock trading typically is done for speculative purposes and therefore has more in common with gambling, investing in stocks is typically performed for longer term capital growth and is more akin to saving. Stock investments have also traditionally been made to hedge against inflation, which is one of the more compelling reasons to invest in stocks.

A number of additional reasons exist for an investor to want to invest in stocks. One of the more common motivations is that stock investments have a history of outperforming many other investments over a long period of time. A growing segment of the population now invests in the stock market to maximize their money's overall return and to protect the value of their money against inflation.

While trading in the forex and commodities markets generally takes on a more speculative nature for most individuals, stocks can make extremely profitable investments over a longer time frame, depending on which ones are chosen, of course. In addition, some stocks pay out quarterly dividends which give people even more incentive to invest in stocks.

Diversity in the Stock Market

The stock market represents the sum total of all publicly-traded corporations which are involved in virtually all sectors of economic activity. By choosing the right stock investments, an investor can indirectly take a gold position, for example, which they could do by purchasing shares in a gold mine.

Furthermore, perhaps an investor's goals are to earn a competitive rate of return without taking too much risk on a stock. In this case, they might consider investing in electric utilities which have traditionally traded for low dollar amounts, pay out large dividends, trade at low price/earnings multiples, and generally offer investors a high degree of security.

Conversely, an investor might prefer to invest in stocks which have a higher degree of risk, due to greater chances of sharp price fluctuations, since they might desire the possibility of a higher return. If so, a great many choices exist in start-ups and other companies that have prices which are more volatile in nature, of which some Internet stocks can present good examples.

A key principle in money-management with stock investments involves the principle of diversification. Basically, by diversifying one's portfolio and investing in a variety of different sectors of the economy, the investor stands a much better chance of achieving above-average returns.

Criteria for Choosing Stocks for Investments

Many people who invest in stocks want to be in on the bottom. For example, Microsoft shares have appreciated considerably in price since being originally sold in the 1980's, returning in excess of 60,000 percent from those early days. Innovation and market forces also often play a major role in the price of a stock.

Nevertheless, some basic elements are usually taken into account when making investments in stocks. These include such fundamental factors as:

- **Earnings** - Fund managers, investment bankers and other financial experts evaluate stocks primarily on earnings. If a company is performing well, their earnings will reflect this, and in many cases will cause the price of the stock to rise.

- **Capitalization** – the amount of stock issued by the company can impact the price of the stock considerably, especially if the bulk of outstanding stock is in the hands of just a few shareholders or financial institutions.

- **Debt** – the amount of money the company owes and the terms of their corporate bonds will also have an impact on the price of the stock.

- **Insiders** – certain corporate figures within the company will often invest in stocks from their company, as will investment banks and other institutional traders. Knowing who owns how much stock and whether they are increasing or decreasing their holdings can affect the stock price.

Many stock investors are wondering which stock will be the next

Microsoft. Taking your best guess about this is one of the basic tasks involved in stock investing.

How Stocks Differ From Bonds as Investments

Stocks and bonds make up a large percentage of possible investments worldwide. Nevertheless some basic differences between the two allow investors varying degrees of risk. This primarily arises because stocks represent an ownership interest whereas bonds represent a creditor's interest.

The following sections discuss the main differences between investing in stocks versus bonds and the reasons that investors might choose one over the other.

Bonds

Bonds represent money that a corporation, community or nation raise through borrowing. While a large number of bonds are sold for the purpose of infrastructure improvement and other community projects, as well as to fund the massive U.S. national debt, this article will cover corporate bonds and how they compare to investing in corporate stocks.

The primary consideration in a bond investment involves income. A bond can either pay out interest in the form of a coupon, which is redeemable at periodic intervals, or it can be sold at a discount to "face value."

The face value of a bond is the amount the bond is worth. For example, a bond for $100K has a face value of $100K. It also sells at a discount to this price which reflects the interest rate the bond will pay out when it reaches maturity.

Assume, for example, that the $100,000 bond is for a term of 10 years and is selling for a discounted price of $50,000. The bond will pay out $100K at its maturity date ten years in the future. This makes the effective interest rate on the bond 5% per year. This is computed by taking the $50,000 discount divided by 10 years = $5,000 and then dividing that by the $100,000 face value to give 0.05 or 5%.

A coupon bond, on the other hand, will generally sell at face value. Such a bond has coupons attached which are redeemable for a percentage of the face value at periodic annual, semi-annual or quarterly intervals.

Stocks

While bonds offer a steady income on an investment, they do not give the investor the potential for capital appreciation that stocks do. Basically, a stock has no limit as to its potential appreciation.

Another advantage that stocks have over bonds as an investment is the fact that stocks enjoy more liquidity and offer the investor the opportunity to cash in at any time. Depending on the bond issue, liquidating a bond position may have more complications than liquidating a stock position.

Basically, stocks represent an ownership interest in a corporation and this ownership can increase considerably in value, whereas a bond can only pay back money invested as a loan. Accordingly, stocks are inherently riskier than bonds and are subordinated after bonds in the case of the liquidation of the company in bankruptcy.

Diversification

Investors need to be well aware of their goals before allocating funds to different investments. Many professional money managers spread investment risk around by using a combination of both stock and bond holdings in a portfolio in a tried and true investment strategy known as diversification.

Diversification generally protects the investor due to them not having all their investment eggs placed in one basket. Diversifying a portfolio by having investments in both stocks and bonds would therefore make the most sense to many institutional and personal investors. In essence, the amount of risk the investor is willing to take will determine the percentage of capital invested in stocks versus bonds.

For example, those who invested in Microsoft stock versus Microsoft bonds in the company's early days would have seen their investment multiplied by several thousand. Nevertheless, the bond investment in the same company, while returning a high interest rate, could never compete with the appreciation seen on the stock.

Why Companies Issue Stocks

In general, the primary reason why companies issue stock involves the raising of capital. The main source for raising capital for businesses has traditionally been the stock market.

In addition, by issuing stock, a company can spread around its ownership. This helps offset some of the risks incurred in having the ownership of a company held in just a few hands.

It may help to explain several things in order to make the above easier to understand. The rest of this section covers the meaning of capital, debt versus equity financing and the pros and cons for companies issuing stock.

Capital

The first concept one must understand involves capital and how this relates to the issuance of stock. As an example, consider a situation where you intend to open a small business, a restaurant perhaps.

A number of expenditures must be made in order to open the restaurant which includes tables and chairs, cooking equipment, as well as food and other supplies. All of the money used for the purchase of these items is called "capital."

Basically, all of the liquid assets of the business, including the money used to purchase supplies and other items to make a profit, are considered capital. Nevertheless, if you do not have enough money to buy all that is needed, what do you do?

Debt and Equity

In order to solve this problem, companies have two options. They can sell shares of stock which represent equity in the company, or borrowing the funds incurring debt.

When you bought all of the equipment for your restaurant, you effectively made an equity purchase in your business. Equity simply stands for ownership in the business.

Equity in a business is typically referred to as stock. Therefore, in order to finance the purchase of additional equipment for the restaurant you can either:

1. Issue stock which represents a partial ownership in the business, to a friend or family member who would like to participate in the profits generated by your business, or

2. Borrow the money from a bank or an individual which will then usually have to be paid back with interest.

Pros and Cons of Issuing Stock

The advantages to a corporation in issuing stock versus incurring debt include:

- Issuing stock means a company can raise considerably more than it could otherwise borrow.

- The company does not have to make periodic interest payments on loans.

- The company will not have to pay off the principal amount of the loan.

The disadvantages to the corporation from issuing stock include:

- Owners must share their ownership and profits with other stockholders.

- Shareholders have rights inherent in stock ownership, such as voting rights, which can affect the operations of the company.

In general, the advantages to a company of issuing stock, as opposed to incurring debt, far outweigh the disadvantages.

Advantages of Owning Stock for Shareholders

In addition, the purchasing of the stock offers significant advantages to its stockholders. These include:

- Participation in future profits.

- Capital appreciation if the company is successful.

- Voting rights in the corporation.

- Possible dividends.

The shareholders stand to gain if the company turns out to be successful because the stock price will usually rise. As a result, the shareholder will earn a capital gain on the value of the stock which typically increases with the success of the company whose equity they invested in. This is one of the main reasons why people buy stocks.

Furthermore, stock investments have made many people millionaires. For example, the employees of Microsoft who had received stock and reinvested it currently number in excess of 12,000 millionaires and four billionaires since the stock initially went public in 1986.

Common Stock versus Preferred Stock

In the world of corporate finance, stock in a company can take on a different meaning with the word common or preferred before it. The two make up the majority of stock issued from corporations.

What is common stock and how does it differ from preferred? The following sections will describe the differences between common and preferred stock and what these differences mean to investors.

Common Stock

Common stock generally refers to a financial claim to a share of a corporation. These claims are issued by the corporation for the purpose of raising cash to fund expansion or other operations in the company.

The common stock of a corporation initially goes to the founders of the company until they decide to offer it to the public. The reasons for offering their stock to the public typically involves the company going through a substantial growth period in which the company needs additional funds to increase operations.

Once the original stockholders of the corporation decide on selling stock to the public, they are permitted to sell a limited amount of shares according to their articles of incorporation. This is also known as the company charter.

Shares for public sale are commonly known as "authorized shared capital" and are initially offered through investment bankers in an Initial Public Offering or IPO. The IPO is offered on a primary market directly to other participants before being traded in the secondary market which consists of the stock exchange.

Common Stock Rights

When you become a shareholder with common stock of a corporation, you have the right to vote for the directors of the company. In other words, the shareholders get to elect the people that ultimately run the company. In addition, other important decisions involve shareholders casting votes such as a takeover by another company for example.

As a stockholder you are also entitled to any dividends that the board of directors decides to pay out. Furthermore, as a shareholder your liability in the company is limited to the amount of money you paid for the stock.

Preferred Stock

Preferred stock is generally non-voting stock, which means that as a preferred shareholder you are not entitled to participate in electing the board of directors. Nevertheless, preferred stockholder typically get quarterly dividends which are not paid out to common stockholders.

Other features of preferred stock include a higher claim on assets and earnings than common stock since this type of stock has priority over the common stock in the event the company winds up in liquidation.

Preferred stock has elements of fixed income securities because of the fixed dividend while also enjoying the potential capital appreciation which is a feature of common stock.

Convertible Preferred Stock

Certain preferred stock, known as convertible preferred stock is sold with a convertibility option. This allows investors the opportunity to convert the preferred shares into common stock within a specific time period.

In essence, purchasing common or preferred stock depends largely on the investment objectives of the investor. Both types of stocks will appreciate in a bull market. Nevertheless, common stock typically outperforms the preferred.

Preferred stock holds value better in down markets and offers a dividend in many cases, which make it an attractive long-term investment. Which stock works best? It will generally depend on your investment objectives.

How Stocks are Offered to the Public

Corporations have traditionally made their stock available to the public through investment banks which generally assume the initial risk in the stock offering. The way that companies make their stock available to the public is through Initial Public Offerings or IPOs.

Nevertheless, a number of considerations on the part of both the corporation and the investment bank must be accounted for before the stock can be made public.

The Corporate Charter

The first consideration for the corporation is its own corporate charter. A corporate charter is the "plan of action" or blueprint for the corporation's operation. The charter includes such key elements as:

- The general purpose of the corporation,
- The amount of debt the company may incur,
- The founding members and
- The portion of the corporation which the charter delineates can be sold to the public.

This latter portion of the company, usually described as a percentage of the original stock of the corporation, makes up the part which can be sold to the public in order to raise capital for expansion or for other uses as deemed appropriate by the corporate charter.

The Investment Bank's Role

A corporation may be able to sell its stock to a few investors without the aid of an investment bank. Nevertheless, if the corporation needs a large offering to raise a considerable amount of money, then an investment bank generally assists in the process.

To begin with, the company must have a track record and either already be profitable or have a particular industry edge. This advantage might come in the form of a new invention or technological advance that will be able to produce considerable profits for the company in the foreseeable future.

The investment bank will generally examine the company and its business prospects thoroughly before underwriting any stock for the company. Underwriting refers to the purchase of stock which the investment bank does initially for its own account before redistributing the shares among its clientele first, and then to the general public.

In the case of a large offering, more than one investment bank usually participates. Once the investment banks have decided that the company holds promise, the investment banks along with the company put together a prospectus. This offering document is then distributed by the participating banks to their clients.

The Prospectus

The prospectus consists of all the pertinent information about the company that any potential investor would want to know. These might include:

- The nature of the company's business
- How long the company has been in business
- What sort of earnings the company has had while in operation
- The amount of stock offered and at what price
- The day of the initial public offering
- The amount of debt on the company's books
- A projection of future earnings

Once prepared by the investment bank, prospectuses will then be offered to the investment bank's customers. In addition, a press release will be issued by the company stating the date and price for the Initial Public Offering or IPO. Customers of the investment bank will generally be the first to obtain the stock before it subsequently trades on an exchange or in the OTC market.

IPOs and How to Find Out About Them

Initial Public Offerings or IPOs are one of the most sought after, and in some cases, the most lucrative ways to invest in stocks. Basically, an IPO is made when an established corporation decides to offer part of the company to the public.

IPOs come in many sizes and for a wide variety of corporations. Nevertheless, getting in on an IPO may not be as easy as one might think.

Many investors do not get the opportunity to invest in an IPO for several reasons, and the main reason is usually not having the right brokerage account.

Finding Out About an IPO

Generally, finding out about an IPO does not require anything more than a watchful eye on the financial news. Many IPOs are announced well in advance of the offering, since it is in the best interest of the company going public to alert as many people as possible.

While the IPO may be announced, often the date and initial offering price will not be disclosed until the investment banks underwriting the stock have completed their analysis and have arranged with the company to bring the stock public.

Investment Banks and IPOs

Most, if not all, public offerings of stock involve one or more investment banks, or merchant banks, as they are also known. The investment bank basically makes the IPO happen by "underwriting" the stock. Underwriting refers to the purchasing of the majority of the stock offered by the investment bank which then has its sales staff redistribute the shares to their clients.

In many cases, more than one investment bank takes part in the IPO, selling what shares it can to their clients. It might then retain a portion of the stock as an investment or for trading in the open market.

The Initial Public Offering Itself

When an IPO is ready to take place, customers of the participating investment bank or banks will receive however much stock the investment bank allows before the stock begins to trade on the open market. The offering price is used before the stock starts trading and is the price that the investment banking customers get.

Once the stock has been distributed among the investment bank customers, it is ready to trade freely on an exchange. The price of the stock can swing wildly in both directions on its initial trading date as the supply and demand factors for the stock have yet to be determined. Nevertheless, many IPOs finish with the stock trading higher than the initial offering price, and much higher in some cases.

How to Participate in an IPO

The only way to participate in an IPO for the initial offering price is to be a client of an investment bank. Only these clients are offered the initial offering price before the stock is openly traded on an exchange.

Typically, a client of an investment bank will receive a notification about the IPO from the investment bank well in advance of the offering. The investment bank will then send their customers a "prospectus" on the company. This is a detailed report which has been extensively researched by the investment bank prior to the IPO.

Once the client has received the prospectus and has decided to participate, they have the opportunity to buy a pre-determined amount of stock depending on the size of their account. Often, a limit to the amount of stock a customer may buy is included in the customer's order form.

After entering an order, the client will then receive the shares in their account directly from the investment bank. The stock appears in their clients' account on the day of the IPO and is available to trade immediately on an exchange after it opens, if the client so desires.

Basically, if you want to participate in an IPO, you will have to have more than an account with a discount broker. For this reason, many smaller investors rarely, if ever, get to participate in these offerings. Nevertheless, you can trade the stock immediately after the IPO, once the stock begins trading freely.

Why People Buy Stocks

Buying stocks was once the domain of wealthy investors or professional traders. Nevertheless, in today's world, buying stocks has become a viable and popular investment option for people looking to make their savings grow over time.

This interest in stocks arises in part because of the decrease in the value and purchasing power of money due to inflation. As a result, people in the United States and other developed countries often need to make their savings increase in value in order to have enough saved up for retirement and educating their children.

Few investments offer the liquidity and potential for significant capital appreciation over time that stocks do. Some of the primary reasons why people buy stocks and why stocks have gained such popularity as investment and trading vehicles are covered in the sections below.

Growth

The principal reason why people buy stocks has to do with their expectations for future growth of a company they might consider investing in. Stocks have traditionally outpaced inflation and have become the benchmark investment for individuals looking to achieve growth in their savings.

Furthermore, fund managers are typically rated against the performance of stock indexes like the Standard and Poor's or S&P 500 index derived from a broad based average of 500 large capitalization stocks. Another common benchmark stock index is the Dow Jones Industrial Average or DJIA of 30 major stocks.

Stocks versus Other Investments

Another good reason why people buy stocks arises from the fact that stocks, especially those of small and medium-sized companies, have typically outperformed all other types of investment over a long period of time. A performance comparison of the returns of several investment choices over a period of 20 years ending 12/31/2008 appears below.

Return	Investment Vehicle
+0.67%	Large Capitalization Stocks – the S&P 500 Index
+6.31%	Mid Caps – Russell Midcap Index and S&P MidCap 400 Index
+6.90%	Small Caps – Russell 2000 Index and S&P SmallCap 600 Index
+4.58%	Foreign Stocks – MCSI EAFE Index
+5.69%	Bonds – Long-term Treasuries
+3.50%	Cash

While large cap stocks which have a capitalization of over $5billion clearly underperformed every investment on the list, the best overall place to have had your money over that 20-year period was in the small cap stocks which have a market capitalization of $250million to $1bilion that returned 6.9%. Nevertheless, the stock-related items in the above list refer to stock indexes and not to individual stocks.

Capital Appreciation

When carefully selected by an investor or stock trader, individual stocks can yield a considerably better return. This is especially true of Initial Public Offerings or IPOs which are the manner in which companies offer their stock for sale to the public.

For example, two high-tech stocks that produced phenomenal results were Cisco Systems, which had its Initial Public Offering in 1990 and rose to a peak of a 99,294% return for investors, and Microsoft, which at its peak returned 74,613% since the stock was first issued in 1986.

While Microsoft and Cisco were by far two of the best investments in the 20th century, opportunities that demonstrate why people buy stocks are almost always just an IPO away.

Other Reasons

Other reasons for buying stock might include investing in utilities stocks to receive an income from their dividends. Public utilities like electric companies have traditionally paid large quarterly dividends, and their nature tends to result in limited price fluctuations in their stocks.

These characteristics make utilities stocks a reasonable investment for money that would otherwise be appreciating nominally and collecting a low rate of interest. Other utility stocks that tend to perform like bonds include water utilities and natural gas companies.

Basically, with an appropriate amount of research or the assistance of a savvy stockbroker, an investment in the stock market could be tailored to whatever market objectives the investor has. In addition, an investment could produce outstanding results for the investor that will of course depend on the particular stock chosen.

Nevertheless, investors always need to remember that the stock market has risks associated with it. As can be noted in the return comparison above, the large cap stocks underperformed even cash as an investment. Accordingly, it pays to do some research or get some good advice before jumping into trading stocks with both feet.

What Cause Stock Prices to Change?

Understanding the stock market and what makes a stock's price change is essential if you plan to invest in stocks or wish to understand the workings of modern corporate economics. Many factors influence stock prices, some attributable to the overall stock market, while others having to do directly with the business and industry of the underlying corporation.

Some of the more direct factors that can change a stock's price, both in the initial public offering and the secondary market, are discussed further in the sections below.

The Initial Public Offering or IPO

The initial public offering date could be considered the most important day in the life of a stock. The IPO date generally refers to the first day on which the stock will begin trading publicly, either on a stock exchange or on a closed network like the Nasdaq over-the-counter market.

The stock's price can display significant movements on that important day. While it may stabilize shortly thereafter, the stock price will be affected as the market's expectations for the company's business prospects fluctuate over time.

Stock Price Factors after the IPO

After the IPO, the stock trades freely until it finds an appropriate price level based on the supply and demand in the market. Many factors make up the pricing of a stock. These might include the capitalization, or the amount of stock issued versus the assets and liabilities of the company, as well as the past and future performance of the company in its particular business.

The price of some stocks can be commodity-sensitive, such as a gold mining stock or an oil company. Other stock prices, like those of Intel and Microsoft, tend to move as their corporation's technological innovations and successes become factored into their stock's price.

Furthermore, as a corporation's profits improve, its stock price will appreciate in most cases. This gives its shareholders a profit on their original investment. Conversely, if the corporation's profits fail to meet market expectations or the corporation posts unexpected losses, the price of the stock will generally fall and its investors will be disappointed.

General Market Factors

The stock market's cycle also directly impacts stock prices. If a broad bear market in stocks is underway, even stocks of companies that have a high intrinsic value and are continuing to produce earnings, are sold mercilessly. This can create excellent buying opportunities.

Conversely, in bull markets even stocks of companies that are not doing well will tend to rise due to the speculative psychological nature of the masses during a bull market.

Another important factor to consider is the industry of the company, as well as its competitors and how their stocks are performing. Often stocks that make up an important part of an economic or commodity sector will rise and fall in tandem, as is the case with gold-mining stocks.

Dividends

Many companies of older and more established stocks pay dividends to their investors. These dividends can be paid quarterly or bi-annually, depending on the company, but most companies pay out dividends on a quarterly basis.

When a company pays a dividend, the amount of the dividend is taken off of the opening price of the stock on the ex-dividend date. Also, in order to receive the dividend, the stock must be held on the "day of record" which typically falls two days after the ex-dividend date. The amount of the dividend is paid out on the dividend date which comes soon after the day of record.

While dividends may affect the stock price initially, they then do not usually have much effect on the stock price. Exceptions arise when a new dividend is announced, or a company has suspended payment of its dividend for one reason or another.

Now that the background and basics underlying stock issuance, trading and investing have been covered, the next chapter will help get you started in the process of actually trading stocks.

CHAPTER 2: GETTING STARTED TRADING STOCKS

For those sincerely interested in getting started trading stocks for their own account, the good news is that you can easily start out doing so with even a modest initial deposit by trading equity CFDs as an online trader in a margin account. On the other hand, if you wish to become a professional stock trader working for a major international bank on a top-notch salary, then your chances of success are much slimmer and the competition truly fierce.

As a result, this chapter will focus primarily on supporting the first type of aspiring do-it-yourself stock trader who will be speculating on equity market movements with their own funds or investing in stocks for longer term gain.

A Trader Learning Action Plan

In addition to reading this book, developing expertise in trading shares by practicing and doing online research at reputable websites in the following general areas is highly recommended.

You can also use the following four step learning action plan as a way to direct the progress of your stock trading education:

- **Step #1: Learn Stock Trading Mechanics**

You will first want to make sure you have the stock trading basics under your belt. This means that you have set up an account with a stockbroking firm or an online broker; you have phone access to a stockbroker or an electronic trading platform that can execute transactions; and that you know how to enter and exit stock positions.

You will also need to know about the different types of orders that your stockbroker permits, how to enter them, and when to use them appropriately.

- **Step #2: Learn How Fundamentals Move the Market**

Basically, stock price movements occur in dynamic response to the situations and events either occurring or widely-predicted for the corporation issuing the stock. Fundamental factors that affect a stock's price may include relevant economic data releases, earnings reports, mergers and acquisitions, share issuances, dividends and lawsuits.

As market participants shift their expectations to encompass such new information, and their positions accordingly, the net result is that the supply/demand balance shifts to a higher or lower price for the stock. To accurately predict future price changes, one therefore needs to take into account fundamental information pertaining to both the stock and also to the currency it is most actively traded in.

You will also want to have access to a good-quality economic data calendar with consensus expectations and release times listed for the numbers due to be released and key upcoming events like elections and central bank rate decisions.

It is also a good idea to research online what the relevant economic releases mean to the market, and their relative importance in terms of market-moving potential. Keep in mind that even major stock markets can be illiquid, with wider spreads and sharper moves often seen during the release of important data.

Furthermore, since you probably will not be privy to information about the large transaction flows that move the stock market, you will want to develop an understanding of why those flows might occur and what factors the big institutional investors use to shift their portfolios between market sectors and individual stocks.

- **Step #3: Learn to Trade Stocks Using Technical Analysis**

Due to the fact that your fundamental information flow may be inferior to that taken advantage of by the larger stock market players, one thing you can reasonably be assured of knowing is the current price for a stock and how it has fluctuated in the past. Having a good price charting system, with a reliable historical data stream is vital here.

Armed with that price data information, you will then need to take the time to become proficient at using the many methods of technical analysis can help you utilize this information to predict the overall direction and even the level of future stock prices.

- **Step #4: Develop a Stock Trading Plan and Stick to It**

One of the classic trading adages passed down by seasoned traders to novices learning the ropes of trading stocks is to "Plan your trade, and trade your plan." By using reliable technical analysis signals and other important market observables to set up your trading entry and exit points in an objective way, you can much more easily avoid many of the emotionally-based pitfalls that can blow out margin trading accounts.

Trading equities often becomes a much more enjoyable and often considerably more profitable experience if you can just find the disciple needed to stick to your trade plan.

Now that you have a general sense for what you will need to learn on your way to becoming a successful stock trader, you can start picking up some of the specific details you will need to know to get started trading equities that are discussed in the following sections of this chapter.

How Stocks Trade

Understanding the stock market and how stocks trade is important to anyone who plans on investing or trading in stocks. It can also be of interest to those who wish to understand how modern corporate finance works.

In practice, stocks are traded on an exchange floor, such as the New York Stock Exchange, on an over-the-counter network such as the Nasdaq market, or on an electronic network. Some stocks can also be traded via Contracts for Difference or CFDs that are a form of derivative that is priced based on the price of the underlying stock.

The rest of this section discusses how stocks trade and covers both initial public offerings and the secondary market.

Exchange-Traded Stocks

Stock exchanges were based around groups of financiers that would meet at specific places to trade stocks and commodities that later became the first exchanges. Stock exchanges started in many different cities around the United States, Europe and elsewhere.

They were later centralized to become just the major stock exchanges in large cities where stocks were listed and actively traded. For example, large U.S. cities like New York, Chicago, Boston Philadelphia and San Francisco all have stock exchanges.

With the advent of electronic trading, much of the trading in stocks has become electronic, even on the exchange floors. Many customer orders are now automatically executed on the exchange's trading platform, rather than via the open outcry method.

While a large portion of stock trading execution is now automated on the exchange floors, several basic manual elements of stock trading continue despite the automation of many of the exchange's functions. Typically, the stock exchange operates using a "specialist system." This means that a designated market-maker or specialist gets assigned certain stocks which they will make prices in and match all orders for.

Such specialist market-makers operating on those exchanges generally maintain an inventory in the stock and provide two-way prices on it to others. Their two-way price or "market" consists of both an offered price at which subsequent investors can buy the stock, as well as a bid price at which those investors who already own the stock can sell what they already have or go short.

If a public bid or offer is not available, then the specialist is obligated by exchange rules to buy or sell on their quoted two-way price, even if only for a small amount before lowering their bid or raising their offer for subsequent transactions.

Exchange traded stocks consist of the biggest corporate names in the world and enjoy a certain prestige in being traded or "listed" on the Big Board of the New York Stock Exchange or NYSE. Nevertheless, times have changed, and most NYSE-traded stocks also trade electronically, as well as on other regional exchanges.

Over-The-Counter and Electronically-Traded Stocks

Even though stocks have been traded over-the-counter for decades, the advent of the electronic age has made the over-the-counter market vastly more efficient. It now makes use of electronic trading platforms such as Level II, in addition to the telephone network that stock traders formerly used to trade over-the-counter on.

In addition to the Nasdaq market, a number of Electronic Communication Networks or ECN's also participate in the trading of stocks, such as Instinet for example, which provide an alternative for both OTC and exchange-traded markets.

Online Stock Trading

Over the last ten years, a number of online broking firms have emerged which have evolved into major players in the world of stocks trading. E-trade is one such example. Many other online firms exist today and their success reflects the general trend towards automation and electronic trading platforms.

Basically, stock exchanges are gradually becoming obsolete as traders move to electronic trading formats. Nevertheless, many exchanges continue to have stocks listed and trade electronically even though they no longer have a physical exchange floor location.

Stock trading has evolved considerably over the last thirty years thanks to the rise of computers. The next three decades will most likely see even more technological advancements affecting how stocks trade.

Mechanics of Buying Stocks

Buying stocks involves several preliminary steps that every stock investor or trader needs to know to successfully buy stocks. The first step consists of course in getting a reputable broker.

The first things you will need to ascertain if you want to buy stocks before getting a stock broker includes what your needs are and what type of investing or trading you intend to be doing. The first item can easily be determined by considering whether your needs are for investment purposes or for short-term speculation.

The following sections discuss what a person needs to know about how to buy stocks, including getting a reputable broker and what stocks to consider acquiring.

Getting a Stockbroker

If your needs mean you might buy stocks for investment purposes, and you prefer to delegate the responsibility to your broker and trust them to research and investigate stocks as well as to execute the trades, then you would be better off getting a full-service broker.

Nevertheless, if you plan on doing your own research and your goals are more to profit from short-term moves, then a discount broker might be a better fit. Also, discount brokers nowadays offer impressive trading platforms with charting capabilities, news wires and other useful research tools.

Choosing Among Stockbrokers

Once you have determined whether to go with a full-service broker or a discount broker, you will need to choose from among a fairly large selection of both types of stockbrokers. A few items to consider in the selection would be:

- **Experience** – a good stock broker will have a minimum of experience with other clients, while a discount broker will have been in business for a minimum period of time and have a good reputation.
- **Commissions** – if you go with a full-service broker, commissions will invariably be higher although competitive commissions are a big plus. Discount brokers tend to have much lower commissions.
- **Licenses and Certifications** – A good stockbroker will have passed a Series 7 test and will have certifications from stock exchanges and other institutions they deal with.
- **Fees** – many brokers charge additional fees, make sure you are clear with the prospective broker about this before making a decision.
- **Investment Philosophy** – if your stockbroker has an investment philosophy you find compatible with your own will lead to a better working relationship.
- **Decision Making Criteria** – how the stockbroker makes decisions will directly affect how they advise their clients.

Selecting What Stocks to Buy

After having successfully chosen a reputable broker and adequately funded a brokerage account, you are ready to buy stocks. What kind of stocks should you consider? This can be answered by assessing your trading objectives as follows:

- **Investment** – if your objective in choosing to acquire stocks is for long term investment, consider companies with good growth potential that pay a dividend and that have a relatively stable price history. Electric and public utilities are popular investments for both individual and institutional investors.

- **Speculation** – this type of trading might take a little more effort and attention. If you are inclined to be more speculative, companies which are involved in new technologies or high-tech products will provide ample volatility for short-term speculation.

Regardless of your investment objectives, if you acquire stocks in well selected companies, you can reduce your exposure to inflation risk. Many individuals invest in the stock market and buy stocks in their individual retirement accounts. If you want to buy stocks as an investment, you are certainly not alone.

Trading Stocks Online

Trading stocks was not the same before the advent of electronic trading via the Internet. The only way a person could even get a stock quote was by calling a stock broker, and then you had to be a customer in order to be given a quote.

Today, you can just type the name of a stock into a search engine, and the results will include a link that will provide a price quote on the stock. In addition, a sizeable database with technical and fundamental information on thousands of companies with publicly traded stock can be obtained from many online stock brokers and other information providers.

Trading stocks over the Internet has gained an enormous following in recent years, with thousands of people currently trading stocks online. If you have no previous stock trading experience, many online stock brokers also now offer demo accounts, much like online forex brokers, where you can practice using their trading platform software and trading stocks.

Perhaps the best way to decide which stock broker's platform is best is by checking each one out that appears on your short list of online stock brokers. You will want to look for one that has the most user-friendly package and whose trading platform fits your needs best.

Also, trading online has become so popular recently that even many full-service brokerages now also offer online packages and trading platforms for their clients. This has made trading stocks over the Internet available to just about anyone with the funds to invest and a connected computer.

With the advent of electronic stock trading via the Internet, an investor or trader can now probably implement their stock execution system on an online stock trading platform that may even allow automation. Also, depending on the broker selected, a stock trader may even be able to get a free stock platform to trade on that they can install on their computer or smartphone or use via a Web browser.

If they are planning on dealing via an online broker, then they will probably be trading Contracts for Difference or CFDs rather than the stocks themselves. From a trader's perspective, there is typically little practical difference when it comes to pricing between a CFD and a stock, since the CFD is priced based on the underlying stock's price. Nevertheless, a CFD on a stock is a derivative of a stock and not the stock itself.

The following sections cover what a stock trading platform is, how it is used as a stock trading system and which types of broker might offer a free stock trading platform.

Advantages of Trading Stocks Online

The fact that the Internet provides a world of resources right at one's fingertips makes up one of the best reasons to trade stocks online. With real-time news and information on the financial markets streaming twenty-four hours a day, information related to individual stocks has now become available to investors almost as it happens.

Getting information on the stock market has come a long way since Nathan Rothschild once took advantage of the information obtained from his secret network that Napoleon had lost at Waterloo to make a killing on the London Stock Exchange from those who thought he had instead won the decisive battle.

In addition to the real-time information stream, stock traders can also take advantage of sophisticated trading platforms that online brokers have developed for their customers. Such trading platforms often contain numerous tools and resources which can be extremely useful to stock traders, like price charts, for example.

Stock Trading Platforms

What is a stock platform? Basically, a stock platform refers to trading software from which a trader can get quotes, enter trades, research stocks, draw charts, read news and obtain other pertinent information on a stock. In some cases, traders can even run an automated stock trading system on it.

Most, if not all online stock brokerages provide a stock platform to support their client's trading. Such trading platforms can be either very simple, with only trade entry and quote capabilities like might be seen on a mobile phone trading platform. They can also be very elaborate, with the possibility of researching fundamentals, insider activity, charts, news and other useful features for traders.

Online brokers typically offer a free stock platform for opening an account, and they might offer extra features such as Level II quotes and high-quality news wires for more active traders. Nevertheless, the stock platform is only as good as the trader using it.

A variety of trading platforms are available which are well-worth checking out. Some online stock brokers will even allow you to demo their stock trading platform before opening a funded account. Furthermore, some stock trading platforms now allow traders to input their trading systems in order to automate their stock trading activities.

Trading Platform Features

While stock trading platforms often vary among different online brokerages, they all share some basic features. These features include:

- **Secure Online Log-in** – just about all online stock brokers share this feature and those with premium accounts can often log in to V.I.P. areas not available to other less-affluent customers.

- **Market Watch Page** – online brokers will usually have an Internet page where you can monitor the prices of those you choose among thousands of different stocks. This price information will often include the bids and offers, trading volume figures, and many general stock market indicators such as the different stock market indexes and the number of advances versus declines.

- **Stocks News and Information Page** – almost all trading platforms offered by online stock brokers offer an informational news feed, either from Reuters or from some other business news wire service like AP Dow Jones.

- **Order Entry Page** – once you have funded an account and have securely logged in, you can then go to the order entry page. This is where you will be buying and selling stocks over the Internet. The order entry page will give the current bid and offer in the stock, as well as the size of the market before you enter the order. In addition, you will be asked to confirm if you really want to execute the trade.

- **Confirmation Page** – once you have entered an order for a stock, you will then receive a confirmation if the order is executed. This will usually alert you with a pop-up window which will then take you to a trade confirmation page.

Automated Stock Trading

Automated or algorithmic stock trading has been implemented for decades by professional trading firms, primarily to trade stocks against derivative products such as stock indexes and stock index futures.

Nevertheless, it was not until online trading accounts were made available that the general public has been able to take advantage of automated trading. To implement this, a stock platform provided by stock trading software companies is often used in tandem with the broker's trading platform.

Although the forex and CFD market has the lion's share of automated trading software available to retail accounts, several online stock trading software companies now offer automated stock trading packages. While automated stock trading has not yet been developed to the point that forex and CFD trading robot software has, a number of other options for stock traders are currently available online.

Trading Systems

A stock trading system need not be automated, and they can either be purchased online or developed by anyone that knows what to look for in a stock. The key to developing a profitable trading system for stocks involves first knowing which stocks to trade.

Selecting the right stock depends primarily on what type of trading system will be used. For example, a system can be developed for day trading, in which case the parameters of the system must require that all trades be liquidated at the end of the trading day.

Other trading systems might involve a longer-term outlook on the stocks selected. These might incorporate swing trading and range trading strategies, or even longer-term trading strategies such as trend trading.

Regardless of what trading system a trader decides upon, position-sizing and other money-management techniques incorporated into the trading plan can increase the profitability of the trading system considerably. As a result, these elements should not be overlooked when developing a stock trading system.

Entering Stock Orders

Once you have developed the confidence to become a stock trader after doing your homework in researching the equity market, developing a trade plan and then trading it in a demo account for some time, you will next need to take the plunge and start trading.

Naturally, the first step in doing so will be to open a live stock account with a reputable stockbroker and have the funds ready to purchase the stock you want to buy.

Next, you will need to know how entering stock orders works. The main types of orders used in the stock market are:

- **Market Orders**

    A market order is an order to buy or sell a stock "at the market" or "at best." This means the broker or dealing desk should execute it at the best price obtainable in the market. Usually this will be on the offer side of the market if the customer is buying or on the bid side of the market when they are selling, although this can vary depending on the size of the transaction.

Nevertheless, take note that a market order never guarantees a price, but only that the broker or dealing desk will immediately execute the order. This becomes an important consideration in fast and volatile markets, or when dealing in especially large amounts.

- **Limit Orders**

    A limit order is an order to buy or sell a stock at a "limit" price, which is specified with the order. The order will be filled if and only if the market goes to the limit price and stays there long enough for full execution. Accordingly, you run the risk of the order failing to be filled even if the price trades.

    If the limit order is a buy order, the market price must be offered at the price specified in the order in sufficient amount for execution to be guaranteed. If it is a sell order, the market must be sufficiently bid at the price specified. Limit orders are extremely useful to technical stock traders that have pre-determined entry and exit points dictated by their trade plans.

    Alternatively, limit orders can also be used to liquidate positions. Perhaps a trader holding a long position has the idea that the market will rise to reach a certain price in order to allow them liquidate their existing position at a profit. In this case, the trader can enter a limit order to sell their position at that better-than-market price in order to close out the transaction.

- **Stop Orders**

    A stop order is an order that gets activated when a certain price trades and then becomes a market order to allow the full completion of the transaction.

    A stop order is usually used to protectively liquidate a position, in which case they are often called stop-loss orders. Stops can also be used to initiate positions by trading "breakouts" in price action where technical factors have confirmed an upside or downside market bias.

    Furthermore, stop orders can be either a buy-stops or sell-stops. A buy-stop instructs the broker or dealing desk to buy at the market once the order price, which is higher than the current price, has traded. The execution of this stop order will limit losses if one is short the stock, or will establish a long position, depending on the trader's initial intention. Conversely, a sell-stop will liquidate an existing long position or will initiate a short position once the specified price, which is lower than the prevailing market, has traded.

- **OCO or a One-Cancels-the-Other Order**

    This type of order is especially popular with personal stock speculators trading their own account using technical analysis techniques. An OCO order usually consists of two separate orders to liquidate an existing position, along with a cancellation request for the remaining order if either order is executed.

    Typically, one is a stop-loss order to protect the trading position against possible adverse price movements, while the other is a limit order to take profits on the trading position. If either order is filled, the other order is automatically canceled by the broker or dealing desk.

Stock Options

Options on stocks or stock options confer upon the option buyer the right, but not the obligation, to enter into a contract with the seller at a particular price. Naturally, the option owner pays a price or "premium" for this right, and they generally exercise their right only when it is to their financial advantage.

Stock options have gained widespread acceptance as invaluable tools for speculation, as well as for getting additional income from and managing risk on stock portfolios. Not only is the stock options market actively-traded among institutional traders, but it is also increasingly available to smaller, personal stock speculators, covered writers and hedgers.

Various stock exchanges have offered options for years for standardized delivery dates and strike prices, and options on stock index futures contracts are also available on major futures exchanges.

Characteristics and Pricing of Stock Options

The price of a stock option is in part derived from the price of the underlying stock which gives the option intrinsic value if it will be profitable to exercise. An option also has another type of value called time value that is generally greater if the price is expected to be volatile and with greater time remaining until the option is due to expire. Options to purchase the stock are called "call" options, while options to sell the stock are called "put" options. Dividends also have to be taken into account when pricing stock options.

In addition to specifying which underlying stock is to be bought or sold, further stock option contract specifications may affect their pricing. These extra factors include the:

- Transaction or "strike" price
- Maturity or "expiration" date of the option
- Delivery date of the underlying stock.

Executing and Exercising Stock Options

When it comes to executing a stock option transaction, the parties involved will first specify an underlying stock and the buyer will be granted the right, but not the obligation, to enter into that specified stock in the direction and at the price they require for a fee or premium.

Furthermore, the buyer of a call or put option can exercise their right to purchase or sell the underlying stock either during (for American-style options) or at the end of (for European-style options) a pre-specified time period, the end of which is known as the expiration or maturity date.

Taking and Managing Stock Price Risk Using Options

Not only do stock options and their various combinations offer unique risk profiles to speculators, but they also offer the potential for creating combinations with the underlying that can hedge positions against undesirable market risk. Positions involving combinations involving options of different maturity dates and strike prices can also be taken. This feature allows a strategic trader or hedger to create a customized option strategy and risk profile that precisely matches their particular needs and market view.

In terms of a simple stock hedging strategy using options, a corporation or individual that wants to protect against a decline in a stock price for an anticipated, although not certain, receipt of stock could purchase a put on that stock in the amount of the probable receipt. The maturity date chosen could either correspond to when the stock was expected to arrive or when the uncertainty was likely to be removed and the stock's arrival was going to become an assured.

These desirable characteristics of stock options considerably broaden the range of strategic and hedging alternatives available to the strategic traders, investment portfolio risk managers, and corporate treasurers who use them.

Stock Trading Tips

For most people, getting started as a stock trader involves getting some sound advice from experts about what to do and what to avoid when trading.

Fortunately, the stock market has matured to the point where a general consensus has emerged about the elements necessary for being consistently successful as a trader. What follows are five top stock trading tips for anyone serious about trading profitably in the equity markets over the long term:

1. Get a Good Stock Trading Education

Certainly, reading this book and others written by professional stock traders will be a great initial step to give you an edge as you start out trading stocks. In addition, you will want to start dedicating a certain amount of time each week to educating yourself on how to execute stock trades, how to keep records, and other aspects of trading that are fundamental to your future success.

Novice traders should also study what fundamental information other stock traders are watching in the market to give them a better idea of what news affects the stock market and particular stocks and why it does so. Also, remember to develop a good understanding of technical analysis since it can really help you develop a trade plan. Both of those key analysis topics will be discussed in Chapter 5 of this book.

A number of useful resources for learning can be found online as well as complete stock trading courses. Furthermore, you can participate in online forums and Facebook groups in order to ask questions and get answers from other stock traders. Nevertheless, no substitute exists for getting mentored by a professional trader who can guide you personally as you progress toward developing your own expertise.

2. Plan Your Trades

Once you have obtained a sufficient amount of education about the stock market and have familiarized yourself about the key technical and fundamental indicators seen in the market, you can begin to develop a trading system or trade plan. A good trading system will advise you objectively of the optimum times to initiate and liquidate positions in the market.

Along with a reasonable risk management plan, you are practically ready to trade once you have a good trade plan. Alternatively, if you are going to be trading CFDs, your trade plan can involve creating or purchasing a trading robot that will automatically enter and liquidate stock trades for you. Nevertheless, please be advised that many such robots on the market have a hard time living up to their historical profitability in live trading.

3. Trade Your Plan

After you have developed a coherent trading plan that fits your needs, lifestyle and personality, be firmly committed to sticking to your trading rules in a disciplined way. Basically, humans can all be victims of their own psychology and get emotionally involved while trading, which can thereby result in costly mistakes.

Typical trading discipline errors include: getting too greedy when taking a profit; doubling up on losing trades instead of cutting losses; and letting winning trades turn into losers. If you do make mistakes, make sure you learn from them by keeping a detailed trading journal and analyzing it periodically.

4. Pick Trades With a High Probability of Success

Your trading system should have an optimal risk/reward ratio as part of its criteria for each and every trade recommended. Your chances of success as a trader over the long term can be much better when carefully selecting trades with a high probability of success.

For example, you can aim for trades with an estimated risk/reward ratio of 1 to 2 or 1:2, which would mean that you plan on risking one unit to make two units.

5. Manage Your Money and Risks Appropriately

Money management has consistently proven itself to be crucial to successful trading over the long term and will be discussed in detail in Chapter 6 of this book, along with the related topic of risk management.

Furthermore, one of the most important things to learn when trading is to avoid over-extending your trading account by taking more risk than is appropriate for the amount of money you are trading with. In general, good money management practices include limiting your losses with stop-loss orders and allowing your profits to run by using trailing stops, which can also improve your risk/reward ratio.

Basically, doing your homework before you start trading can save you both money and emotional turmoil. It can also give you the confidence you need to become truly successful at trading. Hopefully, following these stock trading tips will also help you improve your trading experience over time even if you lose some money initially.

JAY AND JULIE HAWK

CHAPTER 3: ABOUT STOCKBROKERS

A stockbroker is a regulated professional person who is usually associated with a stock brokerage firm or a broker-dealer. Stockbrokers buy and sell stocks and other securities for both institutional and retail clients via a stock exchange or sometimes in the Over the Counter (OTC) Market in exchange for a commission or fee.

In the United States, stockbrokers must pass certain exams to be fully licensed and qualified to deal with the public. The following section covers why a person might need a stockbroker if they are interested in trading or investing in the stock market.

Why You Might Need a Stockbroker

In today's world of investing and speculative stock trading, getting a stockbroker may have its advantages. Many people that have full-time jobs would prefer that a competent and qualified professional do the research necessary to ensure their investments are made in quality stocks.

Nevertheless, if a person has a background in finance or has done the research necessary for their personal investing, they might find that a discount broker or an online brokerage account might be sufficient for their purposes. If so, this will save them considerable money that would otherwise be paid out in commissions and fees to a full-service broker.

What Qualifies a Person to be a Stockbroker?

If a person decides to trade stocks, they must be either members of the exchange the stock trades on, or they must trade through a stock broker that is a member. Most brokerages which deal in stocks maintain such memberships or are associated in some way with the Nasdaq, the New York Stock Exchange or an Electronic Communications Network or ECN like Instinet.

Furthermore, in order for a person to become a stockbroker, a certain level of education such as a Bachelor's or Master's degree in business or finance may be helpful, although it is certainly not necessary.

In the United States, the qualification process for becoming a stockbroker generally involves passing the two exams which must be taken in order to be certified by the Securities and Exchange Commission or SEC which regulates the securities industry. The exams are called the Series 7 and the Series 63 or 66. Passing these extensive tests will allow the broker to become qualified to solicit your business, give you investment advice and execute stock orders on your behalf.

While a broker may perform all of those duties, remember that the stock broker is not a securities analyst, regardless of whether or not they do their own research. They instead act more as a salesperson soliciting your business that earns a commission every time you trade through their brokerage.

Full Service or Discount Broker

The first consideration when selecting a stock broker would involve the type of trading or investing the person is interested in. For example, if you have been trading stocks for a good period of time without the assistance of a full-service broker, you probably do not need the research and other services that a full-time stock broker provides.

On the other hand, some people have an occupation which precludes you from taking the time to research different stock opportunities for their portfolio. In this case, you might be better off with a full service stock broker, although a full-service stock broker will generally ask for a larger initial deposit than a discount broker.

Furthermore, while you may pay much lower commissions with a discount stock broker, you will usually not receive any of the research the large brokerage house offers. You will also probably not be able to participate in special stock deals such as Initial Public Offerings or IPOs which discount brokers seldom offer to their clients.

Basically, your level of investment know-how, the type of stock trading or investing you plan to do, and the funds you have available to invest will determine whether you should to open an account with a full service brokerage or a discount stock broker.

Different Types of Stock Brokerage Firms

When it comes to trading stocks, several options exist for the investor and speculative trader with respect to stock brokers. Knowing what your objectives are as far as trading or investing are concerned will help determine the best type of stock brokerage firm for your personal needs.

The sections below discuss the different types of stock brokerage firms available for trading and investing in stocks.

Investing versus Trading

The first consideration for the type of stock brokerage firm that would be the most suitable for your needs involves knowing whether you are primarily looking at the stock market as a place to invest funds or as a place to speculate.

The stock market comprises one of the few financial markets that can equally accommodate short-term speculators as well as long-term investors. Nevertheless, knowing your primary financial goals will facilitate your selection of an appropriate stock brokerage firm.

If your primary goal in opening a stock brokerage account is to speculate and trade throughout the trading day, whether day trading, range trading or trend trading, a discount broker with a comprehensive Internet interface for facilitating buying and selling might present a reasonable choice.

Conversely, if your goals are more long-term, and you need to invest money which you are not currently using and you want to earn a higher rate of interest than on a T-Note or bond, a full-service stock broker might be a better choice than a discount broker.

Discount versus Full-Service Stock Brokers

Only a few years ago some very marked differences existed between discount and full-service stockbrokers. Nevertheless, with the increase in electronic online trading today via the Internet, many services once only offered by full-service brokers are now also offered by discount brokers.

By the same token, many large full-service brokers now offer customers online access to their accounts through their own trading platforms from which clients can also trade without calling their stock broker directly.

Both types of brokerage accounts have their advantages and disadvantages; however, these depend on the type of investment goals you have. The first and probably the most prominent difference is the commission schedule.

A full service broker will generally charge a much heftier commission than a discount broker per transaction. The reason for this involves their large staff overhead, which involves paying out salaries to individual stockbrokers, analysts and support staff which discount brokers often do without.

Nevertheless, many discount and online brokers now offer extensive online research for their clients, as well as other services that were at one time only offered by full-service brokers.

Online Stock Brokers

In the past fifteen years, the number of online stock brokers operating via the Internet has grown to include many traditional stock brokers, as well as banks and full-service multi-market brokers.

Online stock brokers also no longer just execute stock trades for customers. These days, many such brokers offer a wide array of investor services which might include: mutual funds, bond and options trading, banking, commodities, futures and forex trading, in addition to their stock broker services.

Internet stock brokers can vary widely in the commissions they charge and the services they provide. Accordingly, it makes sense to know what you can afford, as well as what you need with respect to trading and other services which the brokerage might offer. An overview of online stock trading and some of the top online stock brokers and the features their websites offer follows in the sections below.

Online Stock Trading

In addition to full service and discount stock brokers, the advent of the Internet has made a large number of online brokerages readily accessible via your connected computer. Most of these online brokerages offer a trading platform which allows the user to enter stock orders, receive confirmation of trades and manage their portfolio.

Nevertheless, the majority of these online stock brokers do not offer the research which a full-service stock brokerage does, nor do they provide the ability to participate in IPOs or other types of special investments. Also, you will not receive the personal service and advice of a professional stockbroker, but will instead need to deal with the online broker's customer service representatives who often lack a stockbroker's expertise.

Basically, your objectives as a trader and investor will determine whether you will need a full-service broker or if you might be better off with a discount or online broker. Another very important factor to consider is the amount of money you plan on managing. A large amount of money might be better off being placed in a full-service account to obtain the better advice and diversification of funds that such brokers often provide.

Top Online Stock Brokers

Despite the number of new online brokers currently executing stock orders for customers, the current top stock brokers usually consist of the old guard of original brokerage companies which were the first to go online. These top brokers include:

- **Fidelity** – while not the first online brokerage, Fidelity has nevertheless been in the mutual fund business for a long time and offers customers check writing abilities and an ATM card. In addition, your cash balances are invested in your choice of several different mutual fund accounts.

- **E-Trade** – one of the original online stock broker companies, E-Trade offers many features which include stock research, charting and Level II quotes for premium accounts. E-Trade also offers mutual funds, checking and an ATM card, as well as lower commissions for active traders.

- **Charles Schwab** – another of the early online stock brokers, Charles Schwab has grown to resemble a full-service brokerage because of the wide range of services it provides customers. These include managing their client's discretionary accounts and offering the advice of investment professionals. While still a discount broker, Charles Schwab's commissions have also come to resemble those of full-service brokerages.

- **OptionsXpress** – a premier options trading site, OptionsXpress also offers trading in just about any type of financial instrument. This includes stocks, mutual funds, exchange traded funds or ETFs, futures and indexes. They basically provide a one-stop trading shop.

- **Vanguard** – a major name from the mutual fund world like Fidelity, Vanguard makes a good stock broker, in addition to helping you manage your cash. Having a brokerage account with a mutual fund company like Vanguard allows you to consolidate your finances.

- **Thinkorswim** – a relatively new online stock broker, Thinkorswim was started by Chicago option floor traders and offers many advanced features which many professional traders find useful. Barron's has rated Thinkorswin highly and it is a top broker choice among seasoned traders.

- **Wells Fargo** – some are surprised to learn that this bank is also a top online stock broker, as well as offering all of the financial services that a bank typically provides. Wells Fargo offers five different account levels that give you the option of having a straight trading account or a combination of a trading account along with a managed account.

Basically, having a good idea of what you are looking for in an online stock broker firm will help you decide on the best broker for your overall investment or trading needs. Every stock broker mentioned above has some points which are stronger than others and so might make it a better fit for the purposes you intend to open an account for.

What Stock Broker is Right for You?

The decision of which type of stockbroker would fit your needs most appropriately really depends on you. Many smaller traders these days are opting for the easy and accessibility of online trading. Still, if you feel better talking over your investment ideas with a financial professional over the phone, then a full-service account makes perfect sense.

In addition, a full-service broker will often be able to advise their clients of an IPO or Initial Public Offering which the majority of discount brokers still will not be able to provide. Also, the full-service brokerage will also usually allow you to allocate funds not invested in stocks to a variety of interest-bearing mutual-funds which will provide you with additional passive income.

On the other hand, if you do not really wish to discuss your financial investments with a professional and like to do all of your own research on the stocks you trade, then there is really no point in paying the extra commissions that full-service brokers will charge.

If you still want to participate in IPOs and other investment products offered by the full-service brokers and occasionally obtain investment advice, you may want to open two accounts, one with a discount broker and one with a full-service broker. This strategy gives you the best of both worlds.

How to Open an Account with a Stockbroker

Once you know what type of stock investing or trading you will want to be involved in, you must open an account with a stockbroker unless you plan on becoming a member of a stock exchange yourself.

Stockbrokers generally fall into two main categories: discount brokerages or full-service brokerages. An additional category of online brokerages has recently become widely available via the Internet.

The following sections discuss the essentials of opening an account with a stockbroker and what the investor needs to know before opening an account.

Opening a Discount Brokerage Account

Opening an account with a discount stockbroker is perhaps the easiest and cheapest way to get started trading stocks. Most discount brokers also now offer an online stock trading platform where you can enter trades and receive confirmations right on your connected computer which acts as a terminal.

To open an account, all that is needed besides identification are the funds you wish to allocate to your stock trading, and these can readily be transferred directly from your bank account using a bank wire or check.

Many brokerages do not accept cash since they need a physical check for bookkeeping purposes.

Opening a Full-Service Brokerage Account

On the other hand, opening a full-service brokerage account generally involves a bit more than just providing the funds and your ID. Since you will be dealing one-on-one with a stockbroker, you will often need to inform the broker of the general nature of your financial dealings in order to allow them to advise you on the most prudent and suitable investments to meet your financial objectives.

This might involve you and your spouse, if applicable, sitting down with the stockbroker and going over all of your current and past investments. Generally, the broker will look for an overview of your investing history, as well as a complete assessment of your present investment objectives and the level of risk you are willing to assume with the amount of money you intend to place in the full-service brokerage account.

Compiling this detailed information would help give the broker a good idea of how best to proceed with satisfying your particular investment needs

Different Types of Accounts

Three basic types of accounts can be opened for trading stocks with a stockbroker. These accounts types consist of:

Cash Accounts

All brokerages offer cash accounts, whether they are discount stockbrokers or full-service. Basically, a cash account is just an interest-bearing account in which liquid funds are kept in order to buy stocks.

A full-service broker will allow customers up to three business days to pay for stocks that are purchased, depending on the broker's policies. Three days after the purchase is the "settlement date" for stock trades and accounts in good standing are allowed to use this three day time frame to transfer funds if the account is initially not sufficiently funded for the stock purchase.

Margin Accounts

Trading stocks on margin means the brokerage will extend credit for the purchase of stock, often up to 50% of the full value of the purchase. This allows for leveraging of stock positions up to 2:1 and will give the investor a much larger return on their stock investments, if they choose stocks that appreciate of course.

The downside of this leverage manifests if the stock or stocks head South thereby even possibly prompting a "margin call" which happens when the amount of money in the account is insufficient to cover the declining value of the margined stock position.

The way that margin calls are generally handled is by the client either depositing more funds to cover the losing position or liquidating the margined trade. If the accountholder does not deposit additional funds or liquidate, the brokerage will generally do it for them to prevent excessive losses from accumulating in the client's account.

Discretionary Accounts

A discretionary account allows a stockbroker to place trades in your account without having to notify you in advance. In general, this type of account is not advisable unless you trust the broker with your life, not just your money.

The reason for this is that such accounts run the risk of having an unscrupulous broker "churn and burn" the account. This involves the broker trading excessively in order to generate commissions until the account is drained from all of the commission charges.

In essence, giving anyone discretionary control over your finances is tantamount to writing them a blank check. As a result, discretionary accounts are best avoided if at all possible.

Choosing a Reputable Stock Broker

When choosing a stock broker for trading equities, you will want to be sure that you select a reputable stock brokerage firm that will provide the best and most appropriate service available for the funds you have to deposit.

Remember, high brokerage fees and an inadequate trade execution service can be very costly in the fast-moving stock market. The rest of this section discusses some common questions that should be answered during the process of choosing a reputable stock broker.

The following sections of this article list several areas that include key account, security and trading considerations that you will probably want to investigate further before selecting a stock broker.

Each section also includes appropriate questions to ask on various important issues in order to get the answers you will need to make a better-informed decision when choosing a reputable stock broker.

Key Stock Trading Issues

- **Performance** - What is the stock broker's reputation among their clients, and do they provide fast and accurate stock trade executions?

- **Broker Type** - Is the stock broker a full-service stock broker that will assist you with making investment decisions and which offers you special research and opportunities like IPOs, or are they a discount or online stock broker with lower commissions?

- **Trading Platform** - If the stock broker permits online trading, do you like the broker's trading platform and does it have the functionality you require, including supporting any automation needs you might have? Does the broker offer mobile trading solutions and alerts if you need such services?

- **Securities Offered** - Which securities does the stock broker generally provide an execution service for? For example, do they let you trade stocks, penny stocks, futures, indexes, bonds, options, etc?

- **Leverage and Margin** - What sort of maximum leverage ratio does your broker provide (a typical ratio is 2:1 for stocks), what is their margin call policy, and do they automatically stop trades out if insufficient margin is in your account?

- **Stock Trading Fees and Commissions and Broker Loan Fees** - What trading fees and commissions does the stock broker charge and under what conditions? Also, what broker loan fees are charged for shorting stocks?

- **Order Types and Slippage** - What types of orders does the stock broker support? Also, if your chosen trading strategy requires one-cancels-the-other (OCO) orders or trailing stops, does the broker offer these? Does the broker guarantee that stop loss orders will be executed at the price they are placed at, or are you subject to order price slippage in especially active markets?

Key Security Issues

- **Regulation** - What sort of regulation is the stock broker subject to, in what country and under what regulatory agency? Stock brokers are regulated by the Securities and Exchange Commission in the United States. Make sure that this agency regulates the stock broker you choose if you will be trading U.S. stocks.

- **Fund Safety** - Is the stock broker well-capitalized, do they separate client funds from their own in case of bankruptcy and deposit them with a well-rated financial institution, and are client funds insured against loss?

- **Data Security** - If you are considering an online stock broker, you will probably be making personal financial transactions via the Internet or storing vital trading and account information online. In this case, you will want to know whether the stock broker has suitable protective measures in place to keep your data secure from loss or theft.

Key Account Issues

- **Account Types** - Will the stock broker open an account of the type you want with the funds you currently have available to invest? Does the broker offer margin and discretionary accounts if you need them, in addition to cash accounts?

- **Deposits and Withdrawals** - Does the stock broker support making deposits and withdrawals using methods that are convenient for you, and what fees are involved in doing so?

- **Banking Services and Mutual Funds** – what kind of interest do cash accounts earn and are mutual funds available for investing cash balances? Many brokers also offer banking services like checking accounts and credit and debit cards for their client's accounts.

CHAPTER 4: STOCK TRADING STRATEGIES

When it comes to being successful as an equity trader, having the presence of mind to develop a strategy, the mental agility to act quickly in the face of opportunity, and the discipline to stick to your plan is priceless.

Research even indicates that the strategic trading mindset is the optimal way to approach trading in virtually any financial market. The following sections will cover some of the most popular stock trading strategies so that you can get a sense for which general style might suit you best.

If you feel especially creative, then you can always develop your own strategy, but it will probably still help you to know which ones many traders have previously used successfully.

Day Trading the Stock Market

This section covers the very popular stock trading strategy of day trading, including what day trading in the stock market entails and what strategies are commonly used by day traders.

Day trading will generally suit well those traders who do not like to hold positions overnight. In fact, "short-term is noon" could aptly describe a day trader's frame of mind. Basically, being a day trader, whether in the equity or any other market, means that a trader does not take positions home with them.

Each regional stock market has trading hours that you will need to familiarize yourself with by visiting the stock exchange's website. A "day trader" in the stock market really only trades during a specific time frame, which usually encompasses the normal business hours of the main stock markets in their country. Instead of looking at the big picture, the day trader focuses in on what takes place in the market on the day they trade, not tomorrow and not in a month, but just for that day.

Furthermore, certain times of the trading day may seem more advantageous for day traders than others, depending on the stock involved and the strategy they employ. For example, some stocks often see several hours of higher volatility during the hours that London's business hours overlap with those of New York.

How Day Traders Trade

Typically, a day trader aims to take advantage of one or more intra-day swings in the market, usually getting in and out quickly. Depending on the trading system they use, the day trader will often try to capture one or more intraday swings.

Since day traders look to capitalize on small moves, the day trader needs volatility in the market to make their trading activities worthwhile. Fortunately, the stock market lends itself superbly to the needs of day traders and provides ample volatility for day traders to profit from in many major stocks, as well as in the more illiquid secondary stock markets.

Furthermore, day traders generally rely on technical analysis to determine optimum entry and exit points on price charts. The most commonly-used charts for a stock day trader are the five-minute, fifteen-minute and one-hour price charts. Of course, many day traders use a variety of other indicators depending on each individual trader's strategy and trading plan.

The way that a day trader will decide on taking a trade usually involves a particular technical indicator or market signal that, once reached, will prompt the trader to take action. As in most effective trading plans, the day trader will optimally initiate an equity position with clear profit objectives and risk tolerance levels.

To implement this strategy, the trader will generally enter both a stop-loss order to limit their risk, as well as an order to liquidate at a profit once the market attains their objective. Naturally, they will need to cancel the other order once either level is reached, and can sometimes do this automatically with an OCO or one-cancels-the-other order type.

Who Day Trades?

Day trading will not be especially popular with the faint of heart, since the intra-day stock market swings can be stressful to some people. Nevertheless, they usually sleep well at night because they have closed out all of their trading positions by then.

Now that small accounts can be readily opened with online stock brokers and CFD trading is also available, more and more personal equity traders find day trading to be a profitable pursuit.

Range Versus Trend Trading Strategies

The debate over range versus trend trading strategies has adherents on both sides in the equity market, and both strategies have been proven to work extremely well for some people. Since markets sometimes range and sometimes trend, using a combination of the two strategies that are each applied when appropriate can be quite profitable.

The old market saying: "The trend is your friend," describes the general mindset for trend trading, while range trading can be more suitable for shorter-term traders who like to "buy low and sell high."

This rest of this section contains an explanation of range versus trend trading strategies and how stock traders can use either or both trading styles successfully.

Trend Traders

Trend traders typically have a trading style where they first identify a particular trend in a stock's price after a reversal. They then look to subsequently liquidate the position either before the end of the move or just after it ends and reverses slightly. Accordingly, the trend trader will wait for the next price reversal and will follow price movements closely using different technical indicators to alert them of a pending reversal in price direction.

Once identified, the trend generally needs to be confirmed before taking a position. Upon confirmation, a short or long position is established in the direction of the trend along with orders to liquidate the position at pre-determined profit and risk levels.

Often, trend traders will manage their risk by cutting losses and reducing the size of their trades during periods of high volatility in the market. While trend trading is a popular stock trading strategy, and many people use it successfully, it is not for everyone.

Furthermore, in the stock market, money deposited in brokerage accounts can often be leveraged at a ratio of 2:1 which means with $100 you can control $200 worth of stock. Using this sort of leverage, trend traders can make a good deal of money quickly if they catch the right timing on a substantial market trend. Nevertheless, trends can fail and trading on the wrong side of what looked like a trend can be a costly venture when you are employing leverage.

Range Traders

In contrast, range traders typically look for non-directional markets that are forming consolidation patterns. As the name implies, their trading style involves trading within a particular price range.

Generally, they will add to long positions at the lower end of the range and increase short positions at the higher end of the range. They will then take profits as the market approaches the opposite side of the range.

A range trader's view on the market is that regardless of where the price is headed, it is bound to return and trade at the same price eventually. Typically, a range trader will prefer to start with an initial trade and then might add to that position if they see a better price using a "doubling up" strategy.

For example, the range trader might start by shorting IBM near what they think is the top of the range at $155 and then continue shorting it at intervals of $5, until the price reaches a point near the bottom of the range in the $130 region. When IBM's share price subsequently moves down to $130, the trader will cover the entire short position for a profit.

Trading in this fashion could be extremely capital-intensive however, and would require deep pockets in order to trade comfortably. A solution to this dilemma is that many stockbrokers offer clients the ability to trade in fractions of a stock instead of the customary whole numbers. This is especially useful for smaller traders when a stock has a very high price per share.

Trading in fractions of a share makes each penny of the share price worth proportionally less and can substantially relieve the pressure of laying out large amounts of money in margin calls to maintain an underwater position. Basically, by correctly sizing their trading units based on their risk tolerance and account size, a trader can range trade with a smaller amount of money and a lower level of risk.

The Importance of Discipline and Your Trading Plan

While both strategies differ considerably in style, the stock market can accommodate both systems depending on the particulars and parameters of the trading system implemented.

Furthermore, trading style takes second seat in terms of importance when compared to having discipline and a sound trading plan. Either strategy can work for a disciplined trader with a well-defined system. The key seems to be sticking to a trading plan that works and adhering strictly to any planned stop-losses.

Basically, irrespective of whether you use range versus trend trading strategies, having success when trading depends on your skill in knowing how to plan your trade and your discipline when you trade your plan.

Stock Swing Trading

Stock swing trading has proven itself popular as a trading strategy among many equity traders over the years. The stock market lends itself particularly well to short-term strategies, and so swing trading can suit traders looking to capitalize on moves in that market that last more than one day.

A swing trader typically looks for price moves of shorter duration, and they will tend to hold a position for one to five days, although in some cases they might stay in a trade for several weeks. This contrasts with a day trader who generally will not hold positions overnight. Swing traders often use a number of different market signals and technical indicators to evaluate the optimum entry and exit points in the market.

This rest of this section will outline some of the more popular stock swing trading strategies and compare swing trading to other stock trading strategies.

Swing Trading Strategies

The way that most swing traders evaluate the market depends on levels of support and resistance commonly found within a major trend. Such traders generally wait for a stock's price to hit resistance or support levels within the major trend. They might then initiate a new position or add to an existing one once confirmation of the price direction has been made. After such confirmation, the trader will attempt to initiate the position supported by the momentum of the market's resumed direction.

Another swing trading strategy might involve trading against the major trend in the short-term. Such a trader will watch the stock price move into either a support or a resistance zone in one direction, and they then will take position that will profit from the stock price's correction of the initial move. Stops will usually be placed beyond the identified support or resistance zone.

Traders often find swing trading systems relatively easy to develop. A technical analysis plan based on levels of support and resistance, perhaps combined with two other indicators to confirm the short-term trend, are often all a trader needs. Kept simple, swing trading can be relatively easier to manage than day trading, but it requires the trader to maintain a disciplined approach.

Swing Trading versus Trend Trading

Swing traders have a somewhat different outlook from trend traders because they will often look to capitalize on price moves contrary to the major trend. On the other hand, trend traders generally look to identify a trend and establish positions on that side of the market to profit from it. Also, trend traders typically hold their positions for a considerably longer period of time.

A trend trader will simply identify the major trend and initiate a position in that direction. A swing trader, on the other hand, will generally identify a trend and watch as levels of support and resistance become clearly defined.

After the swing trader has established levels of support and resistance, a confirmation by another set of indicators is often required before they initiate a trading position. Typically, the indicators might be exponential moving averages or EMA's and/or a certain reading criteria for the Relative Strength Index or RSI. Once the direction has been confirmed by their chosen indicators, the trader will then initiate a position.

As in all good trading plans, swing traders will place stop-loss orders to control risk in the event they were wrong. They may also place an order to liquidate the position in order to take profits at one or more appropriate levels.

The Grey Area

Swing trading occupies a grey area between day trading and trend trading with respect to trading frequency since traders employing it tend to trade less often than day traders and more often than trend traders. Furthermore, the trading strategy could make a good fit for newer traders and seasoned traders alike.

Although the profits earned with swing trading may not be as large as with trend trading, the strategy generally does not require the amount of activity that day trading requires so stock trading commissions may be saved.

Overall, swing trading definitely merits further study and consideration for those willing to take on the risk of holding trading positions overnight.

Scalping and Market-Making Stocks

Many professional stock traders operate in the equity markets using strategies known as scalping and market-making. While market making is typically unavailable to the retail trader, some exceptionally quick-witted stock traders do manage to find success using the scalping strategy.

Still, scalping and market-making in the stock market can both be risky trading strategies without the proper amount of discipline. Although both types of stock traders mainly look to capture the bid/offer spread, the primary difference between them lies in the size of their transactions and whose account they trade for.

The Dealing Spread

In the stock market, as in just about any financial market, bid and offer prices are constantly quoted in the major stocks to accommodate both buyers and sellers. The difference between these prices represents the bid/offer spread, the dealing spread, or just the spread.

In stock market jargon, "making" or "capturing" the spread means buying the stock at the bid side price and selling the same stock at the offer side price, regardless of in which order the transactions get done.

Market-Makers

A professional stock market-maker, who is sometimes a specialist employed by a stock exchange to make prices in stocks, will usually provide both sides of the rate, or "make a market" to those wishing to deal via stock exchanges.

Over the counter stock market makers may quote prices to their professional counterparties or customer dealing desk or via electronic broking systems. Irrespective of where the trade will take place, a market-maker's primary interest lies in trading on either side of the price because they look to capture the difference between the bid and offer, i.e. the spread, by buying on the bid side and selling on the offer.

While the width of a market maker's dealing spread will tend to be fairly consistent, except perhaps in especially volatile or "fast" markets, their price levels will generally favor one side or the other, depending on whether they are more interested in buying or selling based on their current position. For example, if they are already long, they will tend to show a lower offer and bid, while if they are already short, they will tend to show a higher offer and bid.

While scalpers generally work for themselves, a market-maker can work for themselves, for an exchange as a specialist, or for a bank or another large financial institution which guarantees the market-maker's trades. In the stock market, a market-maker can handle multiple stocks.

Making markets in stocks seems relatively easy in comparison to scalping. A market-maker simply quotes both sides of the stock price, skewing the market they quote based on their outstanding position, and either they or a clerk keeps a running book of their trades. They also aim to lay off any excessive risk with other counterparties, much like a bookie.

While some market-makers operate as independent traders working for their own account, most stock market-makers work as salaried employees of stock markets or large financial institutions, and this tends to takes some of the pressure out of this highly active form of stock trading.

Scalper Trading Methods

Scalpers usually look to capture the spread like market-makers, although scalpers usually are also day traders who trade for their own account. As a result, they trade in much smaller amounts than the large sizes professional market makers typically deal in. Despite their smaller transaction size, scalpers trade the bid/offer spread in much the same way as market makers, usually looking for a quick turnaround on a position.

In essence, scalpers look to get in and out of a trade as fast as possible with a profit. Many scalpers rely extensively on technical analysis to pick optimum times to scalp the market. Generally, the scalper will use one minute, five minute and fifteen minute charts to base their trades on.

In addition to using very short-term price charts, many stock scalpers use WMAs or weighted moving averages. Such scalpers might look for resistance in an upwards trend or support in a downwards trend that shows up as a double top or double bottom in the weighted moving average. Once this signal manifests, a scalper can then begin initiating positions since the price will tend to oscillate back and forth between the moving averages.

Another popular technique used by scalpers involves trading at the opening or closing of major stock markets such as the New York Stock Exchange open or the London Stock Exchange close. Many stock scalpers also use other technical indicators such as Exponential Moving Averages and Bollinger bands to provide trading signals.

Regardless of what techniques a scalper uses, they usually need to be completely absorbed in watching the market and ready to pull the trigger on any given trade. While scalping may sound easy, few trading strategies are more challenging and require as much concentration, discipline and intense trading activity as scalping.

Using Automated Stock Trading Software

A relatively recent development in trading the stock market involves the use of new technologies like automated stock trading software. Such programs are especially well suited to trading Contracts for Difference or CFDs on stocks or stock indexes in online trading accounts available from stock brokers via the Internet. This means just about anyone with even a small amount of money to put at risk can now begin trading in the stock market just like the professionals whose expertise is programmed into these often fully-automated algorithmic trading software programs or "trading robots", as they are sometimes called.

Due to its ease of use, automated trading software has become increasingly popular in recent years, and the advantages it offers for both experienced and inexperienced stock traders are considerable.

Electronic and Automated Trading

Electronic trading has been around for quite some time now and has its origins in the equities market where open outcry-style stock exchanges have gradually given way to automated trading systems that started to become a force to reckon with in the 1980's.

Furthermore, the advent of online trading via the Internet in the past twenty years has brought electronic stock and stock index trading to the masses. In the past few years, automated stock trading software has become increasingly popular, and for good reason. The main advantage that automated stock trading programs provide is that the so-called "trading robot" software truly makes stock trading effortless.

You do not have to watch any screens, have a background in stock trading, do any exhaustive research on economic or corporate fundamentals or review technical indicators to initiate a trade. The automatic trading software comes pre-programmed by stock experts to analyse the stock market using objective and effective technical analysis techniques and optimized parameters.

The stock trading robot then determines entry and exit points, sizes its positions appropriate, initiates a position automatically, and then places liquidation orders. All of this is done completely automatically, without you having to lift even a finger! The only thing you have to do is keep your trading account funded if the live trading results do not show the impressive profits found on the robot vendor's sales page.

The MetaTrader 4 Trading Platform

With respect to online trading platforms that support automated trading, one especially popular option is known as MetaTrader 4. Also called MT4 for short, this platform is even offered for online download at no charge by its developers MetaQuotes.

MT4 provides the data and trade execution facility for some of the most popular trading robots available to online traders. Not only can you purchase an off-the-shelf robot to trade automatically for you using MT4, but you can even use MT4's proprietary MQL 4 programming language to develop your own Expert Advisor or EA to trade a custom trade plan for you.

Getting Your Trading Robot Started

These days, most automated trading software works as an Expert Advisor within an online trading platform like MetaTrader 4 that then interfaces with an online stock or CFD broker that holds your margin account.

To get started trading automatically, you will first need just a few minutes to purchase, download and install the trading robot software of your choice in the directory of a compatible online trading platform on your computer.

The next important step will be to open and fund a trading account with an online stock or CFD broker. Once the funds hit your trading account, you can start your robot running.

The trading robot then advises your trading platform when to initiate a trade based on the pre-programmed trading parameters in the software and the market price action it observes. The robot also places liquidating orders to close any initiated positions out.

At this point, you can just sit back and watch the trading robot's performance as it trades tirelessly for you day and night as long as the stock or CFD market is open and your computer remains online!

Recommendations and Reservations About Using Trading Robots

At present, a considerable number of automated trading software packages can be found for sale online. Nevertheless, many of the available packages seem to optimize their parameters using cherry-picked historical data and then make amazing profitability claims, while at the same time providing disclaimers that future profitability may not be as fabulous.

Accordingly, it can really pay to do some research of your own and test any product you purchase thoroughly if you are serious about using automated trading software to trade stocks or CFDs. Also, automated trading robots generally come with programmable variables, and some people have claimed greater success with their robots in terms of profitability by adjusting these parameters.

Another big advantage to automated trading software is that virtually all products made for this purpose are based on indicators used in the technical analysis of market price movements. Therefore, a thorough study of the software and its trading decisions can give a neophyte a deeper understanding of technical analysis and trading strategies. This is a unique form of a market education that they would not have been able to obtain so easily a few short years ago, other than by watching an expert trader perhaps.

In addition, you can get a free trial for many of these software packages and some of them come with a two-month money back guarantee, so you can paper-trade and evaluate the software yourself before you lay out any of your hard-earned cash.

It is strongly recommended that you do a minimal amount of research on both stock trading and trading software before setting up your margin trading account with an online broker and taking the plunge by letting a robot trade for you without supervision. As world-famous stock market investor Warren Buffet once said, "Risk comes from not knowing what you're doing."

CHAPTER 5: STOCK PRICE ANALYSIS

In order to differentiate pure gambling or speculation from strategic trading, a key element involves analyzing the stock market to determine its most likely future direction. Two primary types of price analysis predominate in today's stock market, and they are typically known as technical and fundamental analysis.

Technical analysis focuses almost exclusively on market observables like the price and trading volume, while fundamental analysis looks at the relative economic and political status of the country and industry that a stock issuer is operating in versus another.

Fundamental analysis for stocks also involves performing a detailed corporate analysis, including reviewing dividends, debt to equity ratios, operating margins, stock buyback and issuance programs, and overall business performance. Most fundamental stock analysts will review a company's latest balance sheet for various factors to determine how strong the firm looks relative to others in its market sector and to assess whether or not its stock seems cheap or expensive.

The following sections will introduce each form of analysis, although a very detailed treatment of these important topics lies beyond the scope of this book and is definitely a worthwhile topic for further reading.

Introduction to Stock Technical Analysis

In any introduction to technical analysis, perhaps the first thing a stock trader needs to understand is that fundamental information like economic data and corporate performance results become rapidly priced or "discounted" into the stock price once they are commonly available to market-makers. The saying that technical traders often use to encapsulate this concept is: "Price discounts all."

The art and science of technical analysis assumes the truth of this idea, in addition to making the observation that human behavior in crowds tends to repeat itself. Such behavior shows up visually in the price action of a stock observed over time as market psychology fluctuates between periods of optimism or bullishness on the stock and times of pessimism or bearishness.

As a result of the foregoing assumptions, the trader basing their decisions on technical analysis can ignore all of the otherwise distracting market information. Instead, they can focus their attention on using the stock price and its past behavior to forecast its future direction, often with impressively accurate results.

Some of the more popular technical analysis techniques and a brief description follow:

- **Chart Patterns**

    Another advantage of technical analysis arises from the fact that many so-called chart patterns provide specific "measuring objectives" in terms of price and even sometimes with respect to time when a particular trigger level is broken. As a result, once they identify a reliable chart pattern, the technical stock trader can operate in the market with a considerably greater degree of objectivity.

    In general, chart patterns tend to fall into the basic categories of continuation, reversal or consolidation patterns, depending on how the subsequent price action usually proceeds once the pattern completes itself.

- **Trends and Channels**

    Trends form an especially important class of continuation chart pattern. Technical analysts generally identify an uptrend by a series of higher highs and higher lows in the price, and a down trend by a set of lower lows and highs. Furthermore, sets of parallel lines can sometimes be drawn through the identifying high and low reversal points to define a channel that the price is moving within.

Once the price breaks an established channel in a direction contrary to the initial trend, that event signals the end of the trend. It also sets up a price objective equal to the width of the channel projected from the point of penetration.

- **Support and Resistance**

    By looking at a chart of price movements over time, a technical analyst can identify places where buying interest overcame selling interest to prompt a bullish reversal in price action, or where selling interest surpassed buying interest to prompt a bearish reversal.

    These levels would be known as support and resistance levels respectively, because buying interest supports the price, while selling interest generally provides resistance to a move higher.

- **Technical Indicators**

    Another major area of technical analysis involves using one or more of the wide variety of technical indicators available to analyze price or volume data numerically. Such indicators usually provide clear trading signals that traders often incorporate into their trading plans.

    An example of one of the more popular indicators is the Relative Strength Index or RSI. The RSI gives insight into whether the market is oversold or overbought and hence due for a consolidation or reversal.

    Another classic technical indicator is the Moving Average that smoothes out the price action and provides useful information about the prevailing trend and possible reversals.

Using Technical Analysis to Trade Stocks

When it comes to using technical analysis to trade stocks, a wide variety of choices are readily available that could suit either the novice or more advanced trader.

Some of the more popular of these technical trading choices appear below in approximate order of the complexity involved in implementing them.

Read a Technical Newsletter

Perhaps the easiest way that a novice trader could start using technical analysis to trade stocks would be to start reading a technical analysis newsletter written by expert technical analysts.

This way, they would receive the ongoing directional advice of professionals working in the field. Then, as they read the newsletter over time, they can gradually attempt to replicate the analytical results that the technical pros provided.

Subscribe to a Trade Signal Generating Service

A relatively modern development in stock trading involves using technical trading signal services. These companies generally provide stock trade signals based on trade plans developed by experts who offer them to the public as commercial products for either a one-time fee or on an ongoing payment basis.

You can simply subscribe to one of these services by paying their fees, and they will provide you with technical trading signals. Subscribers generally then have the choice as to whether to take the signals or not and about how much to place at risk on each trade.

Educate Yourself about Technical Analysis Methods

Many good books have been written about technical analysis, including John Murphy's classic book entitled "Technical Analysis of the Financial Markets" that many professional traders consider the best reference on the subject.

Also, the Internet hosts plenty of online educational material on a variety of websites about using technical analysis to trade stocks. Another idea is to read through the help file on your charting software for each technical indicator or charting tool you think you might be interested in using.

Finally, if you happen to have personal access to an experienced technical analyst, then they can probably provide you with some helpful analytical tips to get you started on the right foot when it comes to applying technical analysis to your trading activities.

Obtain a Charting Service

For those who want to start doing their own technical analysis, perhaps the most important thing do-it-yourself technical traders need is charting software. Your essential charting program should not only provide up-to-date prices for stocks you will need to analyze, but it should also feature the ability to:

- View high and low points on the chart.
- Plot bar and candlestick chart types.
- Chart different periods, including hourly, daily and weekly.
- Draw trend lines, channels and horizontal lines.
- Allow chart annotations.
- Superimpose indicators you want to use and read levels.
- Save charts and templates for future reference.

Fortunately, most online trading platforms will include charting and technical indicators as part of its core functionality, along with a database of historical prices for the most popular stocks and stock indexes. For example, MetaTrader 4 and 5 both include excellent charting features and cost nothing to download and use if you wish to use it for online CFD trading via a broker that supports it.

Develop a Successful Technical Trade Plan

By learning from the experience of others, and perhaps also by experimenting with different technical indicators and analysis methods, persistent traders using technical analysis to trade stocks usually eventually come up with a winning trade plan.

Naturally, your trade plan does not have to win every trade it suggests, provided that it generates bigger winning trades than losing trades over the long term. Back-testing your plan over historical price data can help you assess its past success.

Automate Your Technical Trade Plan

As traders advance in applying their technical analysis skills and develop a successful and objective technical trading plan when using technical analysis to trade, many increasingly wish to program a computer to do all of the trading for them so that they can sit back and relax. What was once only a trader's dream has now become possible in reality!

Some novice traders might prefer to use commercial trading robot software for this purpose, but more advanced traders can now either program or have programmed their own personalized automated trading software that can execute deals automatically through many online brokers using trading platforms like MetaTrader 4 or 5.

Trading Using Technical Indicators

Technical indicators rely solely on levels of supply and demand and can give traders experienced in reading them a clear picture of where the market has been. Nevertheless, technical indicators can only give a probable sense of future direction, not a guarantee.

The rest of this section covers the most popular technical indicators for traders and gives an overview on their usefulness.

Popular Technical Indicators

Most market professionals who take strategic positions will use market indicators regularly to gauge the market and also to base their trading decisions upon. Some of the most common technical indicators used in trading and a brief description of their trading signals follow below:

- **Moving Averages** – a Simple Moving Average or SMA takes the price observed over a period of time and calculates an average price. The SMA will generally lag over the calculation period which is why some technicians prefer to use the Exponential Moving Average or EMA instead. The EMA gives more weight to recent prices relative to older prices and so seems more responsive to price action. Moving averages generate buy signals when a short-term average moves above a longer-term one, and sell signals are generated when the longer-term average exceeds the shorter.

- **Relative Strength Index or RSI** – an index that will indicate an oversold market under 30 and an overbought market over 70 that can offer a trader a sense of when a market might be due for a correction or reversal.

- **Directional Movement Indicator or DMI** – this indicator varies on a scale of 0 to 100 and shows a higher reading when a market trends. The indicator has a positive component the +DI that shows the strength of an upwards trend, and a negative component (-DI) that indicates how strong a downward trend is. The indicator generates trade signals when the +DI and –DI cross. When the +DI exceeds the –DI, a bullish trend predominates, and when the –DI is higher than the +DI, a bearish trend prevails.

- **Volume Indicators** – the volume of trading provides extremely important information to technical traders because it gives indications of how strong a rally or how weak a decline has become. Also, increasing volume often confirms a break out of a consolidation chart pattern.

Learn How to Use Technical Indicators

Learning how to begin trading using technical indicators can be one of the best things a trader can do to improve their results, especially if they are relatively new to trading. Basically, developing a strong technical analysis background can provide both invaluable insights and considerably greater objectivity when trading. As a result, technical analysis provides one of the key elements involved in devising profitable trading systems, with another important component being sound money management.

In addition, with the help of recent technological innovations, a trader can now easily isolate technical indicators, overlay them on price charts, and even program new parameters, often using their online trading platform.

Once a trade plan has been developed, some of the more sophisticated trading platforms with algorithmic trading capabilities can even be programmed to automatically enter orders once conditions have been met based on the technical indicators and other trading parameters specified.

Nevertheless, learning how to use technical indicators for trading makes up just one part, albeit an important one, in the development of a successful trader. Naturally, you will want to avoid the pitfall of using too many technical indicators and thereby complicating your trading unnecessarily. Instead, find the indicators that tell you what you want to know about the market and stick to them.

Generating Stock Trading Signals

Generating trading signals usually involves performing one or more types of technical analysis. Therefore, the first step in learning how to generate signals involves learning about the various technical analysis techniques and how they can be applied to a trading strategy profitably.

Furthermore, a good trading system will not only generate trading signals, but will also give a trader clear indications of where to get in, where to get out profitably and where to admit their trade went wrong so that the position should then be closed out for a loss.

Observing price patterns, technical indicators, and support and resistance levels comprise some of the most common ways to generate stock trading signals, and each of these techniques enjoy a wide following.

Those new to trading need to learn how experts generate trading signals to assist them in trading the stock market profitably. An explanation and example for each of these useful technical analysis techniques appears below.

Chart Patterns

Price charts have been used by traders to forecast the future direction of financial markets for decades. When these charts became readily available to stock traders, many of them would look for classic patterns that would reflect the mass psychology behind the supply and demand reflected in the market's prices.

Most of these patterns have points that, when breached, generate a price objective at which to take profits in addition to a stop loss level. These points in the chart allow traders to take on positions objectively with clear levels in mind to take their profits at and manage their risk of loss at.

This type of signal generation usually requires human interpretation to detect the pattern on the chart in the first place, although computers are getting much better when it comes to pattern detection in recent years. Computers can also offer considerable assistance to traders in both charting the prices and also in calculating the likely price objectives.

Technical Indicators

Perhaps the most popular way of generating trading signals involves using technical indicators, and this has already been discussed in previous sections. Various market observables determine the value of these indicators such as price, volume, historical volatility and open interest, when applicable.

Some of the indicators that a trading system might take into account when generating stock trading signals might include:

- Moving averages – the price average over a set period, for example 5, 10, 30 or even 200 days.

- Relative Strength Index or RSI indicating an overbought market over 70 and oversold market under 30.

- Price action nearing the top or bottom of a Bollinger Band.

The above trading signals comprise some of the more widely-followed and popular indicators. An in-depth study of technical analysis will provide the trader with still other useful indicators that can generate trading signals.

A trading system based on technical indicators usually applies a set of criteria whereby a buy signal, sell signal or do nothing signal would be generated when certain levels are reached.

Support and Resistance

"Buy low and sell high" has often jokingly been considered the prime directive when trading, with the amusing factor being that this is by far easier said than done. Nevertheless, by making a detailed visual study of past price reversal points on a chart, a technical analyst can get a good idea of what price levels on the chart people would be willing to buy or sell at.

For example, the so-called "support levels" below the current market price indicate where traders might have placed purchase orders or simply show buying interest, either to establish long position or to take profits and cover short positions. These levels get their name because they support the market and prevent the market from moving lower.

Conversely, the price levels above the prevailing price where sellers emerge to take profits on long positions or go short the market are commonly known as "resistance levels." They get their name since the price has moved up sufficiently to attract sellers that provide resistance to the market moving higher.

A trading plan could be created to generate trading signals based on support and resistance levels. Such a plan might involve buying ahead of key support levels and selling ahead of where the market finds resistance.

Stop-loss orders could be placed comfortably below the support levels and above resistance levels. Conversely, orders to take profits could then be placed below the resistance levels and above support levels.

Useful Chart Patterns

A number of useful chart patterns can help traders profit from their technical analysis. In general, such chart patterns tend to fall into the basic categories of continuation and consolidation patterns and reversal patterns.

The classification of a chart pattern depends on how the subsequent price action usually proceeds once the pattern completes itself. Triangles present something of an exception because they can break out in either direction, and so can be either continuation or reversal patterns.

These categories and some of the useful chart patterns within them are described further in the subsections below.

Continuation and Consolidation Patterns

As the name implies, a continuation pattern is one that signals that the market price will continue again in the same direction once the pattern has completed. These patterns could also be called consolidation patterns since they tend to represent a pause in the general direction of the market as it consolidates after its recent move.

Volume tends to decrease as the market takes a temporary breather, and it then rises again upon a breakout. Examples of common continuation patterns include:

- **Triangles** – These patterns come in symmetrical, ascending and descending types. The market typically trades in a gradually narrower range between converging trend lines before breaking out on increased volume and continuing in that direction. Although certainly a consolidation pattern, as noted earlier, a triangle can be either a continuation or a reversal pattern, depending on which side its breakout occurs on. Triangles generally consist of five increasingly smaller internal movements, and they must break out before reaching their apex. A breakout sets up measuring objective equal to the width between the converging trend lines that define the pattern at the initial high or low.

- **Flags** - Preceded by a sharp move, often called the "flagpole", the market consolidates between parallel trend lines that often slant counter-trend, before resuming sharply in its original direction, and to a similar extent to the original move.

- **Pennants** – Also preceded by a sharp "flagpole" move, in this pattern the market consolidates between converging trend lines, usually resembling a small symmetrical triangle, before resuming sharply in its original direction and to a similar extent to the original move.

- **Wedges** – Consists of two converging trend lines. A falling wedge pattern interrupts an uptrend, and its breakout is bullish, while a rising wedge interrupts a down trend and its breakout is bearish.

- **Rectangles** – A trading range pattern bordered by roughly horizontal lines drawn among the major highs on the top and among the major lows on the bottom. A breakout in either direction sets up a measured move equal to the width of the rectangle.

Reversal Patterns

Signs of a reversal pattern forming provide a good clue that the market may be about to turn and move in the opposite direction. Examples of common reversal patterns include:

- **Head and Shoulders Top or Bottom** – One shoulder forms, then a head forms a major top or bottom, then another shoulder appears at a similar level to the first. The dips or rallies between the head and the shoulders define a neckline. When the neckline breaks, look for a move equal to the distance between the neckline and the head.

- **Double Top or Bottom** – This pattern forms when two tests of a roughly similar level occur, with an intervening dip or rally. The dip or rally defines the neckline and a break of that level sets up a measured move equal to the distance between the neckline and the double peak or trough.

- **Triple Top or Bottom** – Like the double top pattern, but with three peaks or troughs instead of two.

- **Triangles** – See the previous entry under continuation patterns for triangles which become reversal patterns when their breakout comes in the opposite direction to the preceding trend.

Technical Analysis Software

The term "technical analysis software" used to just refer to programs that charted market price action and allowed traders and technical analysts to draw trend lines and superimpose technical indicators.

Recently, however, the trading world has been transformed by trade signal generator software and other sophisticated computer-assisted algorithms for analyzing price movements.

This article describes some of the basic types of technical analysis software and what benefits each of them offer to the technical trader.

Charting Technical Analysis Software

Perhaps the most important technical analysis software for the do-it-yourself technical analyst will be charting software. Such a program will need to provide real-time prices for each of the stocks, CFDs, indexes, or other equity-related assets you want to analyze.

Such software will probably also include features like the following:

- Plot different chart types including bar and candlestick charts
- View prices on charts and indicators by putting your cursor over them
- Different time periods including hourly, daily and weekly price data
- Ability to plot trend lines, flat lines and channels over prices
- Permit user to notate charts
- Includes a variety of popular technical indicators
- Allows for charts and chart templates to be saved for later use.

Fortunately, most online trading platforms include charting software, and some online CFD trading platforms even allow you to execute trades directly from charts.

Pattern-Matching Technical Analysis Software

Analytical chart pattern recognition software programs of this type often use artificial intelligence algorithms to analyze technical analysis charts graphically. For example, this relatively-recent type of technical analysis software might use advanced pattern-matching algorithms to identify traditional and reliable chart patterns on stock price charts using historical data.

Some of these programs even indicate how certain they are about the pattern, as well as what its trigger points and objectives are. Other programs of this type focus on implementing specific charting techniques like those involved in Elliott Wave Theory analysis, for example.

Although these pattern-matching programs probably cannot yet outperform an experienced human technical analyst, they can usually help a novice identify common chart patterns and compute measuring objective targets, as well as alert an experienced trader to possible trading opportunities.

Trade Signal Generating Software

Now available from several commercial vendors, trade signal generating technical analysis software has become increasingly popular of late. Although the software generally falls short of actually executing the deals it recommends for you, it usually provides an audible signal along with a trade recommendation including information like:

- Which asset to trade
- In what direction to take the trade
- Where to liquidate the position at a profit
- Where to close the trade out at a loss if the market takes a turn for the worse.

In practice, trading signal generation software programs typically review one or more of the popular technical analysis indicators for each of the markets that a trader is interested in. The software then provides some sort of audible or visual signal to the trader when a well-defined trading opportunity is present. The software also usually tells traders in what direction to initiate a position and where to place stop loss and take profit orders.

Automated Trading Software

Trading robot software is a completely automated form of algorithmic trading program that was often considered the "holy grail" by traders of the past, and they usually base their trading decisions on some form of technical analysis.

Nevertheless, most developers would tend to admit that the commercially available trading robot software packages have yet to create unlimited profits for their users without also subjecting them to uncomfortable periods of losses.

A considerable number of software packages are available online with robotic trading abilities that can be set to pick trades automatically. Although automated trading software is admittedly more readily available for the forex market than for stock trading, online CFD traders can also probably use the same software if they are employing MetaTrader as a trading platform.

Nevertheless, many of the more exotic stock investment products do not lend themselves to automated trading because of a lack of liquidity and perhaps also because many such assets are strongly-influenced by key fundamental factors like geopolitical, economic and corporate events that might not be as easy to obtain information about on a timely basis as for a major stock.

Also, many of the automated systems which provide the best results for trading have not yet been released for popular consumption. They are typically used by major investment banks and firms that trade for profit and do not want to lose their edge. Automated trading of CFDs by small retail traders has only recently become readily available, so considerable opportunities for development in that sector exist.

Regardless of whether you seek to trade using a swing, trend or day-trading strategy, a variety of technical analysis software products can provide you with useful trading signals and analytics. While most may not yet be fully-automated for trading, they still can be extremely beneficial in the volatile world of stock trading and may help you watch markets and identify opportunities that you would otherwise be oblivious to.

Why Technical Analysis Works

Those new to trading may wonder why technical analysis works so well to predict future price levels. They might question why just looking at the basic price data or trading volume levels over time can have any predictive value whatsoever. They also might also not understand how to use the various technical indicators that involve quantitatively assessing some aspect of how prices change, or why such indicators can yield useful trading signals.

This healthy sort of skepticism makes perfect sense to novice traders first exposed to the more advanced topic of technical analysis. Nevertheless, many more experienced traders swear by the effectiveness and efficiency of using technical analysis to predict future prices.

As a result, technical analysis has taken a permanent place aside fundamental economic and corporate analysis as an established way of looking at and forecasting future price movements. The rest of this section discusses the theoretical basis for using technical analysis to trade stocks.

An Explanation

Although many people have attempted to explain why technical analysis works, often in quite different ways, perhaps the best explanation arises from the idea that the prices seen in the stock market represent the equilibrium point at which buying pressure equals selling pressure for the equity involved. If either buyers or sellers start to predominate, the price will move appropriately.

Furthermore, the flow of information into the consciousness of the market's many participants tends to occur efficiently as a result of news services and real-time pricing. As a result, the prices seen in the stock market respond rapidly to new economic and political events as they occur, and they even take into account or "discount" events that are rumored to be about to occur.

This means that the prices observed soon discount all of the available information pertaining to each stock, and the prices do this efficiently and on a continuous basis. This general concept underlies what a technical analyst intends to communicate when they say: "Price discounts all."

Why Read the News?

Most personal traders do not have the time, information systems, background or inclination to be reading detailed economic or corporate reports, scanning news wires for the latest news flashes or constantly having their finger on the pulse of the market like a professional market-maker might need to. They generally want to have a life instead.

Using technical analysis can provide a workable solution for such armchair traders. All they have to do is make the reasonable assumption that all such available information gets quickly priced into the market by the trading pros whose job it is to do so.

This really takes the pressure off when it comes to watching the news. Basically, if an information release comes out as expected, the observed price will most likely not change much because the information has probably already been discounted by the market.

On the other hand, if the information release deviates from what is expected, then the market may initially move in the appropriate direction, but then retrace much of its reaction in a somewhat counter intuitive manner.

Furthermore, as the old market saying goes, "Buy the rumor, sell the fact." This often holds true because profit taking typically sets in once the rumored fact actually becomes officially known.

Human Behavior Repeats Itself

Besides the assumption that the prevailing price takes into account all available relevant information, the other fundamental reason why technical analysis works has to do with the repeatability, and hence predictability, of human behavior when people act as a group.

The crowd mentality seen operating in financial marketplaces tends to demonstrate certain patterns of behavior, which in turn show up visually in price movements plotted over time.

Since these observable price patterns tend to repeat themselves time and time again, the results can help forecast the future behavior of market prices. While that may indeed be true, the trick to this form of technical analysis lies in correctly identifying which pattern the market is trading in.

Using Fundamental Analysis to Trade Stocks

Fundamental analysis of a stock generally involves going over the corporation's balance sheet, financial records, debt to equity ratio, and price to earnings ratio. Some analysts may also review relevant data for the sector, including economic indicators, government fiscal policies, social and political factors, and interest rates.

Furthermore, since market prices represent the equilibrium balance point between supply and demand in the stock expressed in a particular national currency, the resulting price also reflects the stock's value relative to that of the currency in which it is quoted.

As a result, fundamental data relevant to that quotation currency can also be reviewed by an analyst when attempting to predict directional movements for the stock's price. A related factor is that some international corporations have foreign operations and may have considerable exchange rate risks as a result when their balance sheets are translated back into their base currency.

Fundamental analysis uses such information as a way of forecasting price trends. While this technique commonly appeals to those traders with an education in economics, business, accounting or corporate finance, just about anyone can learn to determine what fundamental factors move the stock market.

This detailed form of analysis allows stock traders to get a sense of how one stock is valued relative to another similar stock in its sector and to the stock market as a whole. They can then take that into account given the issuing company's future prospects in order to develop a view on the stock's future price.

The rest of this section will describe the basics of fundamental analysis and how to use its techniques to trade stocks.

Key Fundamental Corporate Data

Fundamental analysis of a stock generally involves going over the issuing corporation's balance sheet and financial records. Fundamental traders often pay particular attention to the issuing firm's debt to equity ratio and its price to earnings ratio to see how those parameters compare to other stocks in the same sector in an effort to find under or over-priced stocks.

The release dates of key information about the corporation that issues a particular stock are also closely monitored by stock analysts and traders. Such releases can involve considerable stock market volatility if the actual release differs significantly from the market's consensus expectation.

Key Fundamental Economic Data

The release dates of key economic numbers are widely tabulated in economic calendars. Just like with corporate releases, the precise times when such releases occur can result in considerable market volatility if the actual number released differs significantly from the market's consensus.

The list below includes most of the key economic data releases that reporting agencies within the various countries provide to the market on a regular basis as indicated.

- **Employment Data** – Released monthly
- **Gross Domestic Product (GDP)** – Released quarterly
- **Trade Balance** – Released monthly
- **Retail Sales** – Released monthly
- **Industrial Production** – Released monthly
- **Consumer Price Index (CPI)** – Released monthly
- **Producer Price Index (PPI)** – Released monthly.

Other Types of Fundamental Information

In addition to the aforementioned economic data, some of the other important fundamental information commonly used by traders and economists in performing fundamental analysis might include the following:

- Interest rate levels
- Supply and demand effects
- Political influences
- Geopolitical events
- Growth rates
- Commodity prices
- Survey results
- The Commitment of Traders or COT positioning reports.

Using Fundamentals to Trade Stocks

When performing a fundamental analysis on a particular stock, traders will look at as many fundamental factors as possible for the issuing company and the economy or economies it operates in. They will take all this data into account, as well as the strength of the currency its shares are issued in, when making their trading decisions.

Traders do this in order to obtain a broad sense of what the issuing corporation's internal, economic and political operating climate is, as well as to determine what growth opportunities exist and whether it is suitably valued.

Basically, if the fundamental data looks better for the stock relative to other stocks in its sector, then that would tend to imply a rising forecast for its price if the underlying market is stable or rising. On the other hand, if the stock's data comes across as weaker relative to others in its sector, then a falling forecast would tend to ensue for its market price as long as the underlying market trend is relatively neutral. The stock's price might still rise in a rising market, but probably not as much as other stocks that offer better value. A neutral forecast would tend to result when prospects are roughly the same on balance for the stock relative to others in its sector given their stocks' pricing, as long as the underlying market is stable.

Once having made such a forecast, the fundamental stock trader would then position themselves in the market to take advantage of the forecast movements in the stock's price. Over time, they would update this analysis as relevant news events and data releases occur, and they would adjust their trading position in the stock accordingly.

Stock Valuation Factors

As mentioned in the previous section, the worth of a stock is generally expressed in terms of the currency it is issued in. Accordingly, the price of the stock of a corporation will typically be quoted in local currency terms as well. Furthermore, this market price responds sensitively to long-term economic and interest rate cycles, as well as to shifts in policies and success of its issuing corporation.

Although economic theorists might postulate that stock market price fluctuations form an essentially random walk through time, and some even use this hypothetical assumption when developing theoretical stock option pricing models, for example, almost any cursory review of a chart of a stock price plotted over time will probably convince you otherwise.

Basically, stock prices often show remarkable tendencies to trend in a particular direction over time, often as a response to underlying interest rate adjustments by the relevant central banks. Local inflation rates can also result in persistent underlying market trends that can affect individual stock valuations since stock prices tend to rise overall along with inflation.

Furthermore, the repeatability of the aggregate behavior of large groups of humans often reflects itself in the formation of recognizable technical price patterns that set up reliable outcomes. As detailed in the previous section on technical analysis, many technical stock traders use such patterns to forecast future stock price movements.

Basically, if a corporation is doing well and giving good dividends, then its stock's price tends to rise along with other stocks quoted on a stock market.

Stock Valuation Factors

Many stock valuation experts would agree that the main factor in stock valuation involves the rate of return of the stock in terms of its dividend paid and its growth prospects. Additional stock valuation factors can include such things as:

- Economic growth prospects
- Inflation rate and forecasts
- Trade deficits or surpluses
- What type of credit quality the issuing company has.

Sometimes, a particular stock will be treated differently from other stocks if its issuing company has substantial cash reserves stated on its balance sheet. Such reserves tend to make the stock a safer investment for more conservative investors.

Fundamental versus Technical Analysis for Stock Trading

In terms of the point of separation between the two disciplines of technical and fundamental analysis, technicians rely primarily on market observables like price and volume data, and information derived from those factors, as they evolve over time. Fundamental analysts, on the other hand, take into account just about everything else other than those factors.

Furthermore, when considering the relative merits of focusing on economic fundamental analysis versus technical forms of market analysis many seasoned market pros note some serious issues both with performing fundamental analysis and also with its effectiveness as a technique for forecasting future stock prices.

A discussion of some of their more common concerns and issues with using fundamental analysis to trade stocks follows.

Fundamentals Take Time

When it comes to performing an analysis to obtain a stock price forecast, a fundamental analyst usually has to review a far greater set of information than the technical analyst.

For example, a fundamental analyst might have to look over the company's balance sheet, any relevant news and recent insider trading activity. They might also review a slew of economic data for the country where the stock was issued, as well as take into account general economic factors like interest rates, inflation rates and sector growth. They might also want to look at supply and demand effects, trader positioning, political influences, geopolitical events and relevant commodity prices.

Basically, the complexity of the tasks involved in performing fundamental analysis can get quite daunting. As a result, such fundamental traders can easily get left behind on market moves and stuck deep in analysis paralysis, while the technical traders may have already performed their analysis quickly and moved appropriately into the market in a much more timely fashion.

Lack of Specific Trade Recommendations

Most technical analysts have developed and follow in a disciplined way one or more clearly-defined trade plans. These sets of trading guidelines tell them valuable and objective information about what to look for, when to enter the market, and at what levels positions should be liquidated at a profit or loss.

Technical trade plans also usually incorporate money management principles that tell the trader how to size their trades, generally depending on their risk tolerance and portfolio size. Trading plans will be covered in greater detail in Chapter 8 of this book.

Unfortunately, fundamental analysts usually do not enjoy the advantage of having such clear and objective trade plans to direct their trading activities. It can be difficult for a fundamental analyst to incorporate all of the information they need to review into a specific trade recommendation with pre-defined entry and exit points. The resulting lack of objectivity can often make the difference between a trader being successful or not.

All News is Old News

The idea behind this issue with fundamental analysis is that any news released to the public has pretty much already been noted, analyzed and fully discounted into the stock price by professional OTC market-makers and exchange specialists.

Basically, their intense job requires them to keep their fingers right on the pulse of the market using rapid market data services, news wires and the market's own well-developed rumor-mill.

As a result, traders looking to take positions based on fundamentals will often be sorely frustrated to see the stock price react to favorable news in a thoroughly counter-intuitive way by falling as the market pros "buy the rumor and sell the fact." This happens because the market had already discounted a favorable price move based on the rumor of an event, and so when the actual event occurs, such smart traders will take profits by selling into resulting increased demand for the stock.

CHAPTER 6: STOCK MONEY MANAGEMENT

Trading stocks successfully often has much more to do with what you avoid losing than in making big profits. When trading well by being disciplined and closely following a sound trading plan, money seems to come easily.

Nevertheless, stock traders need to learn to take the good trades with the bad, so using basic money management suggestions like those contained in the sections below can save just about any trader money, stress and frustration.

Basic Money Management Principles

No discussion about trading seems complete without covering the basic money management principles that virtually all successful financial markets traders use and describing how to apply them when trading stocks.

This will be done in this section by explaining a series of maxims that most traders are — or should be — taught before they put actual money at risk in the markets.

- **Never risk funds you cannot afford to lose.**

Since stock trading is more akin to gambling than investing, you will want to avoid trading with your mortgage money or your family's food money. The pressure of placing your hard-earned funds at risk on a stock trade will probably not result in the optimum trading mindset for your eventual profitably.

- **Let your profits run and cut your losses short.**

A time-tested trading maxim, this saying encourages traders to let profits keep appreciating and to take losses quickly. The act of staying in a trade while a market is trending for a large part of the move can be one of the most profitable trading strategies for some. Also, taking losses quickly when you are wrong will avoid having small losses grow into much larger ones.

- **If you can't take the heat, stay out of the kitchen.**

When applied in the market, having excessive heat in your portfolio means that you are probably trading in larger sizes than would be appropriate for the funds in your account, or it might involve some other reason that your trading position is making you lose sleep at night. The point is that you need to feel comfortable with your trading risk.

- **Avoid trading without a stop-loss.**

Because of the volatile nature of the stock market, price moves can sometimes be extreme and dramatic. If you neglect to protect yourself by placing a stop-loss in the market, you risk the possibility that your position may go seriously against you during an unexpected time of high volatility. This can often result in you incurring a larger eventual loss than if you had entered a stop-loss order at an appropriate level in the first place.

- **Never over-leverage your trading account.**

Stocks can be bought with a 50% margin (2:1) which allows you to make more profits faster as a trader, but you can also lose money just as quickly since leverage is a double-edged sword. Use the leverage you will feel most comfortable with if a trade goes against you.

- **Do not give in to greed.**

Greed can get a trader in plenty of trouble, such as running a winning trade into a loss or prompting overtrading and excessive risk-taking. Another market adage goes: "Bulls make money and bears make money, but pigs get slaughtered."

Avoid trying to squeeze the last pip out of a profitable trade since many good traders will tell you they always get out of a winning position too soon. Remember, you will never go broke taking a profit.

In conclusion, remember that taking losses and profits when necessary is a key part of the trading game. As long as a trader can manage risk and employs prudent money management techniques, their losses will be so much less than their winners that they will have little effect on their overall profitability.

Why Money Management is Essential When Trading

When trading stocks or any other type of financial instrument or commodity, using sound money management principles considerably increases your likelihood of success over the long run. The most profitable traders generally rely on money management techniques to ensure their objectivity and clarity when trading.

Traders commonly employ some basic techniques to manage their risk, so the rest of this section will cover the importance of using money management techniques as a stock trader and will describe some of the more popular of money management methods commonly in use by stock traders.

Position Sizing

When developing a trading plan, a trader will determine how much of their account will be put at risk for each individual trade. For example, when trading in a $10,000 margin account, perhaps the trader will risk 1% on each trade.

After 10 consecutive losses of 1% each, the trader will still have roughly 90% of the account's value intact. Now suppose that the trader wants to risk 5% per trade. After 10 consecutive losing trades their trading account would be left with about half of its original value, and the trader may decide to pack it in and go out of business.

On a related note, an important factor when assessing and comparing stock trading plans is the "maximum drawdown" seen with the system over recent market action. This is the most substantial percentage drop from a peak to a bottom, in terms of the account's equity, seen over a certain period of time.

Stop-loss Orders

Most successful traders use stop-loss orders and enter them immediately upon initiating a stock position. A stop-loss order consists of an order to liquidate an existing position at a price worse than the present market price.

Such an order would generally be entered at a level below the level that the position was initiated if the original position was going long. Conversely, a stop would be above the level the position was originally taken, if it was a sale. Performing this important risk-management activity will limit the trader's losses if they enter into a position that subsequently goes against them.

Trailing Stops

A useful money management technique that consists of entering stop-loss orders that have their level scaled upwards if the trader holds a long position that becomes profitable, in order to protect accumulated profits. Similarly, the stop-loss order levels would get scaled downward when the trader has a profitable short position.

Furthermore, if the stop losses on profitable traders are moved to the breakeven point on the trade, this common practice ensures that the trade will probably not show a loss, regardless of whether the market turns, unless order slippage occurs. Then, as the trailing-stop is scaled up or down depending on the position's direction, this will ensure that the trader continues to make and lock in profits while the favorable trend continues.

Risk Management

The importance of risk-management cannot be stressed enough, and one could make a strong case that it forms the most crucial part of a successful trading plan.

Furthermore, a trader should employ risk management techniques that involve taking losses quickly and letting profits grow. This means they can have many more losing trades than winning trades and yet still be successful in the long run.

Basically, the trader and their account will benefit overall from taking a modest number of trades that are much more profitable, even when also taking many losing trades that involved taking relatively tiny losses.

Money Management Mistakes Traders Make

Money management, some experienced traders argue, takes precedence over all other considerations when it comes to trading. Because of the volatility in the stock market, a trader without a money management component in their trading plan could be likened to a skydiver without a parachute. In the event of a string of losing trades, the trader's account will drop much like a skydiver without the benefit of a parachute to slow their fall.

A large percentage of people that begin trading in the stock market fail mainly because of lack of discipline and poor money management. Without knowing how to deal with losing trades, many novice traders start "chasing money out the door" by committing a slew of money management mistakes and eventually losing a lot of money and even their whole initial account balance in some cases.

Some sound advice about how to manage money responsibly when trading has already been given, but it helps to know where the money management pitfalls lie so you can avoid them. What therefore follows are the some of the top money management mistakes stock traders make and how to avoid them to help you stay in business as a trader over the long run:

1. **Not having a money management plan** – as mentioned above, without a money management component in a trading plan, a trader will typically not be able to weather a string of losses.

2. **Neglecting to position size trades** – a good trader will know exactly what percentage of the account will be at risk on any given trade and will not extend trading beyond the limits of the account's funding. Generally, stock traders will risk between 1% and 5% of the trading account's value on any given trade, and by always risking the same percentage, the trader's trade size will grow along with the equity in the account.

3. **Failing to use stop-loss orders** – if a trader does not use stop-loss orders, then they better be prepared for whatever the market has in store for them. Stop-loss orders will save the trader from a modest loss becoming a bigger loss and are a key money management tool. In order to effectively trade with stops, the trader would do well to examine the technical indicators and nearby support and resistance levels and place stop-loss orders accordingly. This helps them maintain a more objective demeanor when trading.

4. **Becoming emotionally involved with a position** – this is a serious

mistake many traders make. Emotional involvement in the stock market can be devastating to a trading account; a trader may insist on holding onto a losing trade simply because they think the market will come back. Yes, the market may come back, but when? Refusing to admit they are wrong and holding on to a losing position will affect the trader psychologically and impair their ability to trade. Emotions are best saved for one's sweetheart and not the stock market. As the market adage states "don't marry your position."

5. **"Averaging" or doubling up on a losing position** – one of the worst mistakes a trader can make involves compounding a loser by adding to a losing position at a "better price" in the belief the market is headed the other way. In effect, the new position would be at a better price thus, averaging the price of two losers.

6. **Failure to take profits** – not taking profits once a trade has run its course can make a loser out of a winner.

7. **Trading with the rent money** – if you can't afford to lose the money you are trading with you will suffer severely in the case of a loss.

8. **Over leveraging the account** – in the stock market, you are typically able to leverage your trading account by a factor of 2 to 1, which is much less than other markets, like forex for example. Still, it makes sense to keep in mind that using leverage can make you more money if you are right but it will also magnify your losses and perhaps even wipe you out if you are wrong.

9. **Letting losses run** – the old market saying is "let your profits run" not the other way around, which can quickly lead to the depletion of your trading account.

10. **Greed** – getting greedy will only get you in trouble. Greed can lead to a number of money management mistakes like overtrading, letting a profit turn into a loss, and position averaging. Remember, bulls make money and bears make money, but pigs get slaughtered.

Common Stock Trading Risks

No section on getting started as a stock trader would be complete without a discussion on the common stock trading risks that can make your business less successful. Trading risk can be defined as the risk of incurring a substantial trading loss or allowing a prolonged trading error to erode the value of your portfolio. All trading involves risk to some degree, and without risk, there would be no potential profit.

For example, volatility, or price swings, is a common stock trading risk, but volatility is also one of the reasons that the stock market can be so lucrative to trade. In essence, it is due to the fact that the volatile nature of the stock market has risk inherent in trading it that the stock markets can provide a handsome return for those willing to take that risk in a disciplined way.

Furthermore, trading risk can be broken down into two basic categories which involve either market-related risk or trading risks that are not strictly related to market conditions.

Market-Related Risks

All market risks relate to general conditions in the economy, the broader stock market, and the corporation issuing the stock. Risk factors that affect the entire trading community interested in speculating on price changes in a particular stock are included in this category.

Common stock trading risks related to market conditions include:

- **High Volatility:** Strong price swings seen in fast markets can trigger the execution of stop-loss orders and may also incur order level slippage when the trade would otherwise have been profitable.

- **Directional Errors:** An error in judgment on the direction of the market that results in the trade being stopped-out at a loss.

- **Illiquidity:** A loss of liquidity can occur when markets are thin that tends to widen bid/offer spreads and can potentially render short-term trading and scalping strategies ineffective.

While directional errors seem almost inevitable, most traders can avoid the other two risks by closing out positions and avoiding trading during fast or thin markets.

Non-Market Trading Risks

This type of risk includes all risks unrelated to market conditions and in particular, those types of trading risks which arise out of trading plan errors or other trader mistakes. The trading risks of this type do not necessarily arise from market movements and can include the following:

- Drawdown risk, which involves having an unlucky string of consecutive losing transactions that deplete a trading account to an uncomfortable level.
- Lack of discipline in following a set trading plan resulting in excessive losses.
- Losing money on price spreads and commissions as a result of overtrading.
- Failing to execute a transaction.
- Forgetting the execution of a transaction.
- Executing a transaction incorrectly, such as buying when you meant to sell.
- Failing to record a transaction.
- Failing to place a stop loss or take profit order on a transaction.
- Erroneous position sizing resulting in taking too much or too little risk on a transaction.
- Failing to diversify your stock trading portfolio.
- Lacking a decisive attitude because of fear of losing money leading to "analysis paralysis," thereby passing up on lucrative trading opportunities.
- Excessive greed in taking profits in a timely fashion, with the possibility of making initially profitable trades turn into losers.

By avoiding this latter group of largely-unnecessary trading risks, a trader stands a much better chance of being successful. Furthermore, this can often simply be done by keeping careful trading and order records, and by adhering closely to a trading plan.

Stock Trading Risks to Avoid

This section should help you distinguish between the stock trading risks to avoid and the risks you want to be taking as a trader. When considering the trading risks to avoid, one first has to acknowledge that a trader generally has to take risks in order to earn a profit trading stocks.

Those juicy, profit-generating risks are absolutely necessary to your trading business, and they do not fall among the group of preventable risks that a trader generally wants to keep away from.

In fact, an important part of becoming a successful trader involves learning how to maintain the necessary confidence in yourself for you to continue to identify and take such risks, even after having incurred some difficult losses.

Stock Trading Risks to Avoid – The Unnecessary Ones

Part of getting constructive experience as a trader involves learning that some potentially-costly trading risks can be rather easily circumvented by carefully managing the trading process as it unfolds. These comprise the category of unnecessary trading risks that will be addressed further in this section.

Sometimes, taking an unnecessary risk can make you an unanticipated and seemingly unlikely profit. For example, perhaps you thought you had bought when in fact you made a transactional error and actually sold, but the market declined in your favor. You were lucky to get out of that error at a profit, but it just as easily could have been a loss.

Unfortunately, you cannot count on unintentional trading errors resulting in such windfall profits every time. The trade could have resulted in a nasty and unprotected loss that could even have wiped out your trading portfolio, especially if you are a smaller margin trader. Any stop loss or take profit orders routinely entered to protect the intended position could instead have magnified the problem given the incorrectly entered trade.

Accordingly, doing what you can to avoid such risky errors and generally directing your risk-taking toward trades that are intentional, have good risk/reward ratios, and accurately reflect your market view will be more likely to keep you in business as a trader over the long run.

Primary Unnecessary Trading Risks

Specifically, some potentially-costly stock trading risks that you want to be aware of and actively seek to avoid when trading include the following:

1. **Loss of Trading Discipline**

This risk occurs when a trader fails to follow the trade plan they have set up for themselves in a disciplined manner. Since the trade plan was designed to keep them within safe trading parameters, the risk of circumventing it is unknown and potentially large. Plan your trade and trade your plan should be your mantra.

2. Overtrading

Some stock traders, especially novices, find executing trades fun and exciting. As a result, they display a tendency to start to trade without a plan or they might trade too often, perhaps taking an excessive number of trades that lack good risk/reward ratios. If such traders do manage to make profits, much of what they earn tends to get eaten up by spreads and commissions. The pros know that it is generally better for the long-term health of their trading business to learn to "sit on their hands" and wait for the good trades to show up than to trade too much.

3. Analysis Paralysis

Some traders succumb to "analysis paralysis" as they get overwhelmed with all of the fundamental information and technical indicators they could be looking at when making a trading decision and therefore fail to act in time to take what would have been a winning trade. While one should definitely avoid overtrading, you will still need to trade sometimes to make money as a stock trader.

If you find yourself watching screens all day without ever trading, then perhaps you need to lower your risk/reward standards and jump into the market to get your feet wet. Practice making and execute trading decisions quickly and incorporate that idea into your trade plan since the stock market waits for no one.

Other Unnecessary Trading Risks to Avoid

Other unnecessary risks to avoid when trading stocks that generally indicate a lack of adherence to your trade plan might include the following five errors:

1. Failing to pull the trigger
2. Jumping the gun
3. Not taking timely profits
4. Moving or pulling stops

5. Entering low probability trades.

Finally, keep careful records of your stock trades, and do your best to confirm each and every transaction you make in order to avoid potentially-costly transactional errors. The same degree of attention and care needs to go into placing the orders you need to have to protect your profits and limit your losses.

While you cannot control the market, you can certainly exercise power over your own behavior. That alone is what often differentiates the experienced trader from the novice and the winner from the loser.

JAY AND JULIE HAWK

CHAPTER 7: STOCK TRADER PSYCHOLOGY

When it comes to trading any financial market, the unique psychological makeup you bring to the endeavor — combined with your mindset when actually trading — can have a very substantial impact on your success and enjoyment of trading.

This chapter will cover some of the basic things you need to know about the psychology of trading so that you can start optimizing your chances for success.

Why Psychology is so Important to Stock Traders

Most traders who wish to stay in business over the long term generally approach their work using a trading plan which they expect to follow closely. Nevertheless, to keep to a trading plan in a disciplined way is not as easy as you might initially think.

Regardless of how effective a trading system might be in theory, the truth remains that a system is only as good as how much discipline the trader using it maintains during its implementation in practice. If the trader only follows their trading system partially, then they will only obtain partial results that will probably not be the results they want.

Nevertheless, some traders permit some flexibility to enter their trading systems. Often, this might come into plan when taking profits, for example. Having this type of flexibility and being able to exercise judgment can even be a key element in such traders' overall success.

The rest of this section will discuss the importance of psychology in the field of stock trading and how successful traders use psychology to maximize profits.

Psychology and Trading

When trading, a trader's mindset and psychology often determines whether they will eventually be profitable. Successful traders usually know that emotions can hurt their ability to approaching their work objectively and that trading errors made due to emotions can even cost them their business.

As they participate in the trading process, a trader can become their own worst enemy if they allow emotions to have any part in determining the outcome of their trades. In fact, studies have shown that a trader's psychological approach or mindset can account for up to 80% of what makes a trader successful.

Reacting to Adversity

For example, knowing how they react in adverse trading situations gives an experienced trader an advantage over a novice trader or a person who has no experience in the field whatsoever.

Consider the case of a trader that has initiated a position which immediately shows a loss. They now have two options:

1. Keep the trade as an "investment" and wait for the market to go the other way.

2. Liquidate the trade immediately and take a small loss.

A seasoned trader will probably either liquidate the losing trade immediately, or perhaps they might hold the trade for a short period until they were sure the market had failed to turn around, maintaining either a stop loss level in the market or in their heads.

A trader with less experience, on the other hand, can often tend to hold the trade without a time or price limit, hoping that the market might turn in order to recover their loss.

The Emotions of Fear, Hope and Greed

The above example illustrates two basic emotions at play in trading psychology: fear and hope. The seasoned trader justifiably fears losing more money and quickly liquidates the position. In this case, they use the emotion of fear appropriately to cut losses and keep them from increasing to an uncomfortable level.

On the other hand, the novice trader relies on their hopeful emotions, rather than on common sense and reason, in thinking the market might turn around. In effect, this allows losses on the trade to grow as the market continues going against the position.

Another key emotion which finds ample expression in the world of trading is greed. This can be defined as the desire to acquire more than one needs or deserves. When trading, giving into greed can have serious consequences, such as failing to take profits when appropriate. This error can often cause a trader to turn an initially profitable trade into a disappointing loss.

Basically, the importance of psychology when operating in the stock market, and virtually any market for that matter, cannot be overstated. Mass psychology is responsible for both economic bubbles, where greed drives a market to unsupportable highs, as well as economic depressions, where fear causes exaggerated selling pressure. A good trader can learn to take advantage of both opportunities by managing their emotions when trading.

The Trading Animal Farm Analogy

It can sometimes help traders understand their own psychology and that of other market operators by drawing an analogy between trader behavior and that of certain animals.

As noted in the previous chapter, an anonymous stock market adage goes, "Bulls make money, bears make money, but pigs get slaughtered." Apparently, this warning was originally intended to remind stock traders to avoid the emotional pitfall of greediness, but it also applies very well to those looking to trade any market successfully.

To take this analogy a bit further, what can be referred to as the stock market's "animal farm" consists of traders who tend to conform emotionally to one or more of the classic animal personalities listed below.

The Bulls

Stock traders who are bulls or bullish on a particular stock tend to charge ahead as they optimistically think the price for that stock is going up, up, up! As a result of their positive perspective, they will take a long position in the stock.

For example, they might believe that economic prospects for the corporation that issues the stock look great or are due to improve significantly relative to those observed for the sector as a whole.

In addition, perhaps interest rates also favor the underlying stock market, so traders long a diverse portfolio of stocks will receive income from the dividends as they hold long stock positions long term. Nevertheless, even strong bulls need to remember that the stock market has a tendency to overdo things sometimes and such excessively-directional bullish optimism can often lead to the resulting bubble bursting sharply as the market moves "up the stairs, but down the escalator" as the old market saying goes.

The Bears

This brings us to the bears. Bears can be grumpy creatures whose sour view on the market gives them pretty much the opposite take to the charging bulls. Accordingly, stock traders who are bears or bearish on a particular stock pessimistically think the price for that stock is going a good way down, and so they will take a short position in the stock.

While it needs to be remembered that stocks that can only be sold short on an uptick in certain exchange traded stock markets, traders can short any stock whenever they can find another market participant they can trade with willing to bid. Bears might take a short trade if they think that a particular company is struggling financially and its prospects are likely to worsen in future sufficiently to go beyond that of the underlying market's often-upwards trend.

Like bulls with their excessive optimism, bears should remember that no downward trend lasts forever, so they need to be flexible enough as stock traders to realize when the market has turned to the upside.

Interestingly, while bulls and bears are perhaps the best-known animals that stock traders tend to resemble as they position themselves in their market, they are not the only ones. This is where the proverbial farm comes in.

The Sheep and the Chickens

The next animals in the stock market barnyard are the sheep and the chickens. Each of these trading animals fails to make money trading stocks because they are both too afraid to take a position, although for slightly different reasons.

The sheepish trader is just too shy to try something new, while the chicken trader is afraid of getting killed when they enter the market. Together, they just sit on the proverbial sidelines, waiting for the perfect trade, which naturally never comes.

Basically, any decent stock trader has to be willing to lose some money in order to eventually come out a winner; neither can they expect to win if they continually override their trade plan and fail to pull the trigger when their plan signals a trade.

Taking no risk means receiving no reward, so these self-sidelined traders might just break even after allowing their fear to kill their stock trading business while they wasted plenty of their valuable time watching screens.

The Pigs

As referred to in the well-known saying at the beginning of this chapter, the next stock market trading animal is the pig. This trading beast tends to succumb to greed and so they refuse to take profits on winning positions when appropriate, as they try to squeeze a bit more money out of the market.

Instead of taking their gains and living to trade again, they might even make the classic trading mistake of allowing their initially winning trade to turn into a losing one that costs them money. Eventually, allowing their greed to rule their trading will lead to the slaughter of the pig's trading portfolio.

Maybe no one ever went broke taking a profit, but plenty of piggish stock traders have gone broke by failing to take one. Pigs also tend to take substantial risks boldly and without doing their homework in impatient attempts to make big, quick profits trading stocks. Unfortunately, they often end up killing their trading business in the process.

Sure, both bulls can make money and bears can make money as the pendulum of a stock's equilibrium price swings to and fro. Even the chickens might be able to peck a few grains out of the market as the other trading animals pick up profits from the greedy losing pigs.

So, after reading this section, ask yourself what kind of stock trading animals will you avoid being?

Emotions Commonly Experienced When Trading Stocks

Few experiences can make a person feel their emotions more intensely than trading an account with their own money in the stock market. Trading can make a person feel on top of the world when making profits but severely depressed when watching their trading account begin to evaporate into thin air.

This section will cover what emotions traders frequently experience and what this can imply for those interested in trading the stock market successfully.

Trading as a Business

Anyone who has ever run a business will tell you that emotions and business do not mix well. Trading the stock market has many similarities to running a business, mainly because people who participate in trading do so to make money, just like most people aim to do with their businesses.

Nevertheless, because of the immediacy of gains and losses in the stock market, people tend to get emotional much more easily than in other types of businesses. Even with the best laid plans, people often tend to break the rules when emotions take over, even if they have made those rules themselves.

Emotions Experienced When Trading

A list of the most common emotions that traders experience when trading and what impact these emotions may have on the trader's account are outlined below:

- **Fear** – one of the all-time market drivers. Nobody trading in the market likes to lose money and fear of losing can have repercussions on both individual traders and the market in general as fear will make markets drop faster and further than any other market emotion. Fear also impedes traders from taking action when necessary and leaves some traders holding losing positions much longer than appropriate, magnifying losses.

- **Greed** – Another major factor driving the markets. Many people do not even realize how greedy they have been conditioned by society and are surprised once they start trading. Greed can be very dangerous to a trader. An old market saying goes "bulls and bears make money but pigs get slaughtered."

- **Hope** – An important emotion that can affect traders' behavior considerably. Hope is generally felt after a trader has taken a trade which subsequently goes against them. In this case, the trader often hopes the market will turn around and make the losing trade profitable. Unfortunately, hope has no basis in reality and can only impair the trader from trading effectively and taking losses promptly to protect their portfolio. Fear of losing more money is a more appropriate emotion in this instance, and the trader should give up hope and just liquidate the position according to their plan.

- **Excitement** – Trading the stock market can be exciting, especially when riding on a wave of winning trades. Nevertheless, such excitement can lead to a number of trading pitfalls that include overtrading and carelessness. Many such overly-excited traders have been surprised to find their account with a net loss at the end of a busy trading day after commissions and spreads have eaten away any profits.

- **Depression** – An emotion that a trader often feels after a string of losing trades, especially if the losses resulted from them not being disciplined. An often-crippling emotion when trading, depression finds better expression when left outside of the trading arena. Most traders stop trading if they find it makes them depressed.

- **Anger** – A common emotion experienced when a trader fails to take a profit and ends up running the trade into a loss. Also seen when a trader makes a losing trade and fails to put in a stop-loss, thus digging themselves deeper into the hole.

Basically, emotional reactions really have their proper place within relationships and not when it comes to trading the stock market. Remember, if trading is going to be your business, you need to treat it like one.

How Emotions Can Impact Your Stock Trading Profitability

When trading in the stock market for your own account, your emotions and how you manage them can become the single most challenging issue facing both new and seasoned traders alike.

Basically, dealing with the intense emotions generated when trading can be daunting to anyone, and so knowing how to cope with how you feel after an unsuccessful trade is as important as knowing when to get in and out of the market.

Furthermore, for most successful stock traders, having learned how to effectively deal with their emotions represents a key element of their success. Attaining mastery over your emotions therefore forms a main part of the ideal trading mindset.

The rest of this section will explain how emotions can directly affect the profitability of a stock trader, and how seasoned stock traders manage their emotions when trading.

Fear

As one of the most elemental human emotions and therefore a key factor in trading any market, fear can either be useful or detrimental, depending on the trader's mindset. In its most useful sense, fear works as a defense mechanism as in the "fight or flight" instinct shared by virtually all higher beings.

When trading markets, fear can affect a person in a number of ways and often finds expression as:

- Fear of failure.
- Fear of missing a trade or missing out on a move.
- The fear of losing profits already earned.
- The fear of impending doom or loss.

While fear can spur a trader to cut losses before they get bigger, the emotion can also impact a trader by rendering them ineffective as they watch losses grow. Such an experience can make the trader reluctant to continue trading and thus result in them missing other potentially-profitable trading opportunities.

Greed

The fictional Gordon Gekko character from the 1986 movie "Wall Street" was perhaps best known for the famous line: "Greed is good." Without debating that controversial point, greed nevertheless constitutes a major part of the stock market's participants' emotional make-up. It can also affect traders in ways that many only discover after they begin trading.

Some of the ways in which greed directly affects traders follow:

- **Failure to Take Profits** – Some traders manifest greed by not taking profits according to their set trading plan. Instead, the trader might hold out for a little extra money, or perhaps see their losses erode as the market turns.

- **Overtrading** – traders often make this mistake in a hurried attempt to make money instead of patiently waiting for optimum trading opportunities.

- **Taking Profits Too Early** – When traders realize their gains ahead of the levels that their trading plan indicates, this often results in a smaller profit than if the original plan was followed. Remember to let your profits run.

- **Taking Excessive Risks** – Greed can also manifest by a trader taking excessive risks in an attempt to make large profits fast. This generally leads to disaster as encapsulated by the old market saying that goes: "Bulls make money, bears make money, but pigs get slaughtered."

Hope

After the serious impact of fear and greed, hope often gets overlooked. Nevertheless, the emotion still manifests and affects traders in decidedly unprofitable ways. In general, hope arises when a trader has a losing trade and continues feeling that they are still on the right side of the market.

A trader in this situation often hopes that the market will come back, but yet this may never occur, prompting the currently losing trade to become an even bigger loser. Eventually, the trader might wind up taking a much larger loss than if they had put in a stop-loss and gotten out right after incurring the initial loss.

Not only do such experiences result in losses, but having such an experience will often psychologically scar the trader by shaking their self-confidence.

Overcoming Emotions When Trading

Overall, emotions need expression when trading, but they cannot be relied upon to make prudent trading decisions and can adversely affect your trading profitability.

As an alternative, maintaining strict adherence to a proven trading plan can provide an excellent defense against giving in to emotions experienced while trading.

Managing Emotions When Stock Trading

Trading the stock market differs from most fields of endeavor in that even the most profitable and efficient trading systems can be sabotaged by the human element. The trader that gets caught up in an emotional whirlwind while trading usually only has a limited time in the business and probably not a pleasant one at that.

Emotions are a natural human response, but every trader needs to learn to manage their emotions in order to be successful. Furthermore, even if a trading system has been proven to work under all market conditions, the system can only be as good as the person implementing it.

Accordingly, if a lack of discipline exists in the trader's approach, it really does not matter how well their system would otherwise perform.

The Psychology of Losing Trades: Cut Losses Short

Trading the stock market successfully often requires behavior that goes contrary to normal human psychology. For example, consider the situation in which a novice trader has made a losing trade but still stubbornly thinks the market is wrong and they are correct. As a result, they decide to hold the trade in the hope that the market will change its direction and eventually allow the trade to return to profitability.

The novice trader's reaction approaches the normal psychological reaction that just about any optimistic person would have in the same situation. Still, it is always better to be right than optimistic when it comes to trading stocks, and as the market saying goes, "Cut your losses short."

Furthermore, this novice trader may have to wait a long time for the market to turn, if it ever does. They may also have to suffer unpleasant margin calls due to the erosion of their trading account in the meantime. This could serious curtail their ability to take full advantage of future moves they would have called correctly.

In this case, this trader would do much better by replacing the optimistic hope of the market reversing, with the fear of losing more money that has far greater significance when it comes to staying in business as a trader.

Unfortunately, most novice traders rely too much on hope than is appropriate when trading, making it considerably more difficult for them to be effective and successful at the endeavor in the long run.

The Psychology of Winning Trades: Let Profits Run

Alternatively, if a novice trader has a trade that immediately shows a profit, the normal psychological reaction might be to liquidate the trade immediately after the profit arises, thereby ensuring a gain. "No one ever went broke taking a profit", as the old saying goes.

Nevertheless, this saying actually contains a hidden warning about how taking losses could clear out your trading account, rather than offering a suggestion to take a profit as soon as you see one. Instead, the preferable market trading maxim to remember when dealing with winning positions recommends, "Let your profits run."

More experienced traders often allow their profits to expand appropriately by entering trailing stop-loss orders at increasingly tighter levels as the market moves in their direction. This technique helps ensure that the trade gets liquidated close to the best possible profit-taking level before the market reverses, not at the first sign of a profit.

The Mindset of a Successful Stock Trader

All truly successful traders share certain characteristics, regardless of what market they are trading or what trading system they are using. One such attribute is their mindset. In this case, a trading mindset refers to the state of mind of the trader when engaged in their trading activities.

The rest of this section will discuss how maintaining a favorable mindset for success, including working from a pre-determined trading plan and following its rules closely, usually notably increases a stock trader's profitability.

Elements for a Successful Trading Mindset

In order to achieve consistent success in stock trading, most experts consider two elements of utmost importance:

1. **Trading Plan** – This is a written set of strategic guidelines for a trader to follow that covers things like how and when trading will take place. Provided that it is well-defined and profitable, the trade plan need not be complicated. In fact, many of the best trading plans are kept simple in order to be easy to follow.

2. **Discipline** – Involves the trader having the willpower to follow their plan. Many traders find this element the most challenging, because emotions often get in the way and incite a trader to break their own rules. In essence, having rules and sticking to them become two entirely different matters when trading.

Furthermore, to develop a constructive trading mindset, a novice trader must be aware that trading can, and usually does, highlight character issues that my not even have entered the trader's awareness beforehand. These issues, such as feelings of unworthiness, can manifest unconsciously as counterproductive behavior during the trading process, thereby causing the trader to lose money.

Have a Trading Plan

Having a solid trading plan, while very important, really only consists of half of the game. Implementing the plan and having the discipline to follow one's own rules becomes the real crux of the biscuit.

Several common errors that traders make while executing a trading plan include:

- Letting greed influence trading decisions and not exiting trades according to the trading plan.
- Allowing fear to impede taking action when the trading plan indicates taking a position.
- Using too much leverage resulting in taking more risk than necessary when trading.
- Enjoying the trading process a bit too much and losing money by overtrading.
- Making costly errors through carelessness in executing trades and placing orders.

All of the above mistakes reflect to some degree the trader's underlying psychological makeup. Furthermore, they can include emotional responses that may not have arisen had the person not started trading.

The mindset of a successful trader will have worked out suitable responses to many, if not all, of these issues and therefore stays more focused on implementing the trading plan rigorously.

Keep a Trade Journal

Keeping a journal which tracks not only every trade, but the emotions generated by each trade can prove invaluable in becoming a successful trader. Such a journal might have the trader's trading plan at the beginning as a reminder to keep to it. It also will ideally detail their emotional responses to both winning and losing trades, with a special emphasis on the latter.

In essence, the mindset of a successful stock trader keeps centered on trading according to their well-defined trading plan and minimizing any emotional responses to their trading activities. This helps ensure that the trader will be as objective as possible and will therefore find their emotions less distracting.

Finally, many traders find that studying the mindset and psychology of other successful traders can prove extremely helpful. Learning from the mistakes that others have already made can save any trader both money and frustration.

Developing an Ideal Stock Trading Mentality

Developing an ideal stock trading mentality does not have to be difficult. As long as a trader is willing to make a commitment to being disciplined in adhering to a well-defined trading plan, achieving the mindset of a successful trader falls well within the reach of all traders.

This section covers the principles and general steps involved in developing an optimum stock trading mentality that will help virtually any trader start out on the right foot or get back on track to success.

Good Traders Have a Plan

Of course, to achieve this mindset goal, finding or developing a trading plan would be the first order of business. Trading systems generally have their basis in technical analysis. For example, they might use technical indicators such as Relative Strength Indicators and moving averages to generate buy and sell signals on which to initiate trading positions.

The Internet provides a number of resources for learning about technical analysis, as well as entire online trading platforms with an impressive array of technical indicators and charting software. Many of these trading platforms have programmable features that can assist a trader in developing and automating their own trading system.

Items to Include in a Trading Plan

A list of four items that would be useful to include in a trading plan to enhance your trading mindset follow:

1. Pre-determined entry points to initiate trades.

2. Levels for stop-loss orders to manage risk after establishing a losing trading position.

3. Levels for take-profit orders to lock in gains after establishing a winning trading position.

4. Position-sizing specifications related to the size of the account and your risk tolerance.

Incorporate Trading Plan Flexibility

For the trading plan to have an optimum level of effectiveness in generating profits, incorporating a certain amount of flexibility in it generally allows for specific exceptions, especially with respect to profit-taking.

This allows a trader to take advantage of unforeseen circumstances and opportunities, without losing their resolve to manage risk effectively on unprofitable trades.

Strengthen Confidence in Your Trading System and Yourself

In order to achieve the ideal stock trading mentality, it can really help to build confidence in your system by seeing its trading performance under back-testing and demo trading conditions. This process also allows you to make any necessary modifications to your system before placing your hard-earned money on the line.

Your success when practice or demo trading will also give you a good idea if you already have the disciplined stock trading mentality necessary to become a successful trader. Also, any success you had will probably also give you greater confidence when placing actual funds at risk.

Furthermore, having confidence in an objective trading plan or strategy by having tested it makes a trader much more likely to execute it with the required discipline. This allows the trader to achieve an optimum trading mentality, and helps makes trading a much less emotional endeavor.

Achieving a Successful Trading Mindset

Generally, achieving the ideal mindset for trading the stock market boils down to having three things in place well before live trading begins:

1. A reliably-profitable and tested trading system.

2. The self-confidence to take action when called for.

3. A sound money management component in the trading system.

These three elements, while not being a guarantee of profitability, will tend to make trading much less difficult and more manageable on an emotional level.

Also, by having solutions already worked out in their trade plan well before problems arise, a trader can stay much more in tune with the market and thereby achieve a level of success that may surprise even them.

JAY AND JULIE HAWK

CHAPTER 8: STOCK TRADING AS A BUSINESS

Many new stock traders who just jump into the market often find it necessary to stop trading for a while in order to figure out what went wrong and why they did not have the success they initially anticipated.

Planning in advance how you intend to run your trading business can be a helpful process to avoid such a potentially painful lesson. Taking the time for such forethought will also start your process of becoming more strategic as a trader, which should greatly improve your chances of success.

Developing a Stock Trading Business Plan

One of the best ways to start developing a plan for your business is to write down a comprehensive guide for you to follow when managing your trading activities.

Doing so can really help you understand your goals when participating in stock trading and can also provide a detailed business plan laying out how you intend to achieve them both to yourself and potentially interested investors in your trading business.

This section discusses how to develop a business plan to increase your chances of profitability when trading stocks.

Writing a Successful Trading Business Plan

Seven suggested steps that you can go through sequentially to develop such a trade plan are as follows:

- **Step 1: Set Stock Trading Goals**
  Describe in detail why you want to start trading stocks, what needs you hope to fulfill by doing so, and how achieving that goal will make you feel.

- **Step 2: Determine Financial Status and Objectives**
  List how much money you have to fund your trading portfolio with, what sort of income you require or expect from your trading activities and over what time frame, and what that will translate to in terms of a percentage increase in your trading portfolio's capitalization over a suitable time frame.

- **Step 3: Trading Psychology**
  Explain your overall psychology when trading, including such items as: how you analyze market movements, on what time frames you prefer to trade, how you feel under a normal range of trading events, and how you plan on managing your emotions while trading.

- **Step 4: Choice of Trade Strategy**
  Discuss the trading strategies that you intend to use, why you selected them, when you are going to use them and what stocks you intend to trade with each strategy.

- **Step 5: Trade Strategy Details**
  For each strategy you employ, describe first how you will enter the market. Then discuss under what circumstances you will liquidate the position, including how you will set stop loss and take profit orders.

- **Step 6: Money Management**
  Provide your money management intentions, including how you will limit risk on each trade and on your account overall. This might include limiting losses incurred in particular time frames, as well as the number of consecutive losing trades or losing days. This section would also describe what you will do if any of these risk limits are met.

- **Step 7: Demo Testing and Live Trading Plan**
  Cover how you will go about demo trading your trade plan, and under what circumstances you will stop testing it, and either scrap the plan or commence live trading using it. Also discuss how you will begin subjecting your trade plan to testing using a live trading

environment in terms of how much of your portfolio you are willing to place at risk initially, and how you might go about increasing that if the plan trades successfully.

Why Develop a Stock Trade Plan?

Putting together a stock trading plan makes sense for virtually any but the most casual and uncommitted trader. By following the above steps to develop a comprehensive stock trading plan, you should gain a greater understanding of your motives and intentions when trading.

You will also start to become far more strategic about your trading activities. That progress alone can substantially improve your chances of becoming a more profitable stock trader when you next decide to place funds at risk.

Plan Your Trades and Trade Your Plan

A very significant percentage of stock traders fail to make money when they first start out trading. Some of these people just take their losses and quit trading, while the more persistent stock traders will often take the time to learn what they did wrong so that they can be more confident about moving back into the market.

One of the ways to develop this confidence is to create a trade plan that describes in detail the circumstances surrounding your trading activities and also details exactly how you intend to execute your trading strategy and manage your account.

You will also want to discipline yourself to properly test your plan, and if the test succeeds, you will then need to execute this trade plan faithfully. In essence, this process is what seasoned traders are referring to when they say: "Plan your trades and trade your plan."

Basically, the advantages of having a trade plan and sticking to it when trading stocks are numerous, so this section will cover that topic and describe the trade planning process in greater detail.

How to Plan Your Trades

The first step toward greater success in trading stocks will often be to take the time to write down a detailed plan for how you intend to run your trading business, including how you enter and exit trades.

Creating such a plan will often include taking the following key steps to:

1. Set your stock trading goals
2. Determine your financial status and objectives
3. Explain your trading psychology
4. Identify your choice of trading strategy
5. Provide trade strategy details
6. Clarify how you will perform money and risk management
7. State how you intend to demo test your strategy and then start trading your plan in a live account.

Before you make your first stock trade or another trade, it really makes sense to take some time to think about your trade plan and put your thoughts on paper.

Trading Your Plan

Once you have developed and tested a workable trade plan, the next step is to implement it. Unfortunately, this part of the process can present considerable difficulty to traders that do not have the discipline to keep to their plan.

Such a loss of discipline might arise if the trader lacks confidence in themselves or their trade plan. It might also happen if the trader becomes overwhelmed with their emotions when trading and allows their own fear, greed or hope to direct their trading activities instead of their trade plan.

While the market sometimes gives such traders lucky breaks, unfortunately, allowing emotions to rule when trading is far more often a recipe for financial disaster.

Advantages of Having a Trade Plan

As you work though the steps toward creating a trade plan detailed in the earlier section, you will gradually be forming a stock trading plan that will reflect your needs, desires and risk appetite.

Furthermore, you will obtain a considerably greater picture of what motivates you to trade and exactly what you intend to do when trading and under what circumstances.

Going through this relatively simple process can significantly advance you toward the goal of becoming a profitable stock trader. It will also provide a considerably sounder basis for having confidence in your trading choices when you next start trading stock.

How a Stock Trade Plan Can Help Keep Emotions in Check

Emotions that arise when trading can be the downfall of any trader unprepared for their potential impact. Developing a stock trading plan to manage such emotions can be the key to trading stocks successfully.

This section reviews the emotions experienced when trading stocks and describes the advantages that having a stock trading plan can provide for managing them more effectively.

Common Emotional Responses Experienced When Trading

When trading an immediately profitable position, human nature leads many novice v traders to take the profit from the trade quickly. This allows them to avoid the fear of losing money and gives the trader instant gratification.

Nevertheless, if the market continues rising, the trader will usually become emotionally frustrated at having taken such a small profit instead of holding out for the higher return they might think they really deserved. Basically, taking small profits and letting losses run large is going to drain such traders' accounts far too quickly.

While the two scenarios above illustrate how normal human emotions can be detrimental to the trading process, subsequent action based on emotional reactions can make matters considerably worse. For example, inexperienced traders have a tendency to get caught up in their emotions and the fun of trading, rather than "sitting on their hands" and waiting for good trading opportunities like the more seasoned trading pros have learned to do.

This causes the novices to start to "overtrade," by taking on stock positions with poor risk/reward ratios and trading excessively. Often, this means a net loss that is further compounded by market spreads and commissions. Although overtrading sometimes results in a pleasantly profitable surprise, it far more often leads to disaster for the trader's account.

Advantages of Managing Emotions with a Trade Plan

Many people have found out the hard way that, when it comes to trading, emotions should be controlled at the very least, and in most cases completely avoided in the decision-making process. The vast majority of successful traders develop a technical system which they incorporate into a stock trading plan to trade the market and maintain a strictly-disciplined mindset with which to approach their trading activities.

In doing so, they avoid the pitfalls of overtrading, early profit-taking and holding onto losing positions. Furthermore, they generally end up sticking to their trading rules and managing their trading account's risk with as little emotional involvement as possible.

Emotion and trading make strange bedfellows and most seasoned traders recommend being as impersonal as possible when it comes to trading. Avoid marrying a position, have a way to determine when you are wrong and know in advance what appropriate protective actions are needed to save your portfolio from further losses.

Also, stubbornness in trading the markets has been the cause of countless serious losses, and it can be a very easy mistake to avoid if you are well aware of the severity of its risk. By developing and strictly following a stock trade plan with a profitable track record that can be executed without much discretion, you will place yourself firmly on the right path to becoming a successful trader.

When to Make a Stock Trade Plan

Ideally, developing a trade plan to help manage emotions would happen before you even make your first trade. Nevertheless, if you have already been trading for a while, but have not yet considered this type of risk or written down a trading business plan, you can still derive considerable benefits from doing so even now.

Basically, producing a business plan will not only assist you in controlling emotions that arise when trading, but it will also help you to review and solidify your personal trading business activities and goals. Also, if the plan looks good, you might even be able to use it to find new investors to trade for!

Business Risk Considerations When Trading Stocks

Hopefully, by now you have either formulated a trading plan or resolved to do so before stepping back into the stock market. Still, while many novice traders and even some experienced traders focus largely on mitigating trading risks, another important type of risk traders need to be aware of and evaluate when reviewing their trading activities is business risk. This can be defined as the risk that your business will fail to have enough funds to cover its costs.

Stock traders need to be just as vigilant about managing business risk as they are about making trading gains since it involves doing what is necessary to stay in the trading business long term. This often means taking a closer look at your trading process from a risk versus reward perspective.

This rest of this section will covers some of the primary business risk-related issues involved in trading stocks that you should be aware of and have a plan for how to deal with them.

Business Risk/Reward Analysis

Performing a risk/reward analysis usually involves taking a reasonably objective assessment in terms of size, timing and likelihood of any risks the business might encounter.

It also involves considering what sort of rewards can reasonably be expected to result from your trading activities and to what size and over what time frame you project them to accumulate.

Also, since some risks are more probable than others, they can be weighted in a risk analysis according to their probability of occurrence, and then multiplied by the potential size of risk or loss involved.

Assessing Business Risk

Specific examples of business risks which traders can encounter, organized in two basic risk categories, appear below.

1. Financial Risks:

When trading, business risk often stems from financial risk that is related to the size and reliability of any debt being serviced so that you can stay in business trading. Business risks to traders can involve the financial risks such as:

- Losing more money trading than you can afford to.

- Displeasing your employer, domestic or business partner by spending time engaged in trading, and who then insist that you stop trading.
- Inadequate or negative returns from your trading activities that induces your investors or partners to withdraw their financial backing from your trading business.
- Having margin calls in excess of your ability to cover them due to an unfavorable market movement.
- Needing to pay interest on trading loans in excess of you can afford.

2. **Economic Risks:**

Economic risk presents another form of business risk which depends on the general regulatory and economic climate that can impact your business as a trader. The following economic risks can be encountered by traders:

- You can no longer trade because new regulations exclude you.
- Trading amounts, spreads or fees exceed what you need to continue to trade profitably.
- The tax code changes in a way that negatively impacts your trading business.
- You are unable to obtain items needed for your success due to insufficient funds or education. For traders, such things might include:
  - trading platforms
  - technical analysis systems
  - account management facilities
  - access to live news and quotes
  - trader mentoring
  - courses on trading, technical analysis and money management techniques.

Advantages of Business Risk Analysis

Assessing business risk by considering what financial and economic risks your trading business might face, in addition to performing a quantified risk/reward analysis is well worth doing and could make the difference between success and failure as a trader.

Also, such a risk analysis can be added to your trading business plan to increase its scope and broaden its perspective both for yourself and for any potential investors you might hope to attract.

CHAPTER 9: PARTING ADVICE FOR STOCK TRADERS

No introductory book about stock trading would be complete without offering a little friendly advice because, while the mechanics of stock trading remain relatively simple, trading equities profitably has never been especially easy.

The basic fact remains that most inexperienced individuals tend to lose money when trading stocks, especially when they start to resemble the less successful stereotypes among the market "animal farm" on an emotional level, as was discussed earlier.

That certainly does not mean that you will also lose money in stock trading, and you might even be lucky enough to make your next fortune speculating in the stock market! Nevertheless, the humbling fact remains that the stock market has a lot more losing participants than winners, so that means you need to start smart when it comes to your stock trading in order to give yourself the best chances of success.

Trading Tips to Take Away

The following set of eight stock trading recommendations come from the authors' own experience of trading equities and other financial markets professionally, both for financial institutions and also for their own personal accounts.

Together, these tips form the concluding section of this stock trading beginner's guide as you embark on your trading journey with a good solid foundation in stock trading, analysis and money management to build upon with your own experience. Anyway, here they are:

- **#1: Get Your Stock Trading Started on a Good Foundation:** Reading this book was a great start for your stock trading career since when learning to trade the stock market, you will first want to develop a good foundation in the mechanics of how the market works, as well as in the details of how to execute stock transactions in your trading account and how to enter orders responsibly. Similarly, always practice trading in a demo or practice account, if possible, before using a live account to test a new trading platform.

- **#2: Learn to Understand Market Moves:** You will also benefit greatly as a stock trader from deepening your understanding of why the market moves. Do your homework and persistently work your way up the learning curve as your stock knowledge base will grow from both a fundamental analysis and a technical analysis perspective.

- **#3: Consider Having a Trading Mentor:** We were both mentored by more experienced traders when we started out as professional risk takers. Most people in the early stages of their stock trading career would benefit from finding an experienced stock trader who can show them the ropes when it comes to trading successfully, and who can answer any questions from their seasoned and expert perspective that might arise in the beginner's mind. Remember that to get the best results from any time spent interacting with such trading mentors you should take the time in advance to prepare high-quality questions for them to answer.

- **#4: Avoid Common Stock Trading Pitfalls:** In fine-tuning your trading process, you will also want to learn in advance what common trading pitfalls you should avoid in order to stay in business as a trader over the long term. Never fail to learn from your own mistakes or from those of others.

- **#5: Keep Emotions Out of Your Trading Decisions:** Since most trading mistakes arise from emotional involvement, remember not to emulate the trading farm animals, and vow to keep greed, fear and hope out of your trading process as much as possible.

- **#6: Develop and Test an Objective Trade Plan:** Instead of trading by the seat of your pants, take the time to develop an objective trade plan that will gradually grow your portfolio. You will also want to avoid subjecting your trading funds to excessive risk that could cause painful individual losses or longer-term draw downs.

- **#7: Plan Your Trade, and Trade Your Plan:** Your trading decisions to enter positions, take profits and cut losses should not be emotionally-based, and your trading responses should be thoroughly planned out before you pull the trigger on opening any position. Learn to follow the steps and guidelines outlined in your trade plan in a disciplined way.

- **#8: Do Not Take Risks You Cannot Afford:** Keep your optimal risk/reward ratio in mind when trading stocks and use it as a yardstick by which to measure each trade plan or individual stock transaction you might consider. Size your positions appropriately, protect your portfolio from excessive losses, and avoid taking any risks that might bankrupt your trading business, and never speculate with money you cannot afford to lose.

Good Luck on Your Trading Journey

If you have read this book from cover to cover, or even just skimmed it to fill in whatever gaps in your trading education remained open when you first picked it up, then you should by now have an excellent foundation for moving forward more successfully and strategically as a stock trader.

Congratulations on getting this far, and may the profitability of your stock trading business exceed your goals and serve its desired purpose in your life.

CHAPTER 10: RECOMMENDED FURTHER READING

As an endeavor, trading goes back to the age-old beginning of commerce. Fortunately, many successful traders throughout the years have written about their experiences and mistakes so that those newer to trading do not need to repeat them.

For further education on the topic of trading, the reader is first referred to the other books in this beginner's guide series that deal with the more advanced aspects of trading and market analysis and are written by the same professional authors.

Beyond that, a broader list of recommended stock trading literature should probably include books on trading in general, because regardless of what market you are watching, traders of every discipline share the same overall experience.

In addition, reading books that focus solely on market analysis techniques like technical and fundamental analysis will give newer traders deeper insights into those disciplines that lay beyond the scope of this introductory book.

Classic Books on Trading in General

The first book on stock trading that comes to mind would have to be "Reminiscences of a Stock Operator" by Edwin Lefevre. Based on the life of Jesse Livermore, this classic book captures the attitudes and mindset of one of the most successful stock traders of the first half of the 20th century.

Although the stock market was still young then, the book still gives you a good idea of what goes on in the mind of a remarkably successful trader.

Two more recent bestsellers provide a useful perspective on trading for aspiring or seasoned traders alike. "The Market Wizards" and "The New Market Wizards" by Jack Schwager both contain excellent interviews with some of the world's top traders. Together, they give extraordinary insight both into the traders' psychology, as well as into how to profit in specific markets and how such top market players developed their trading systems.

Another fascinating book on trading is "The Complete Turtle Trader" by Michael Covel. The book recounts the famous story of the Turtles — a group of traders that were trained in trend-following by master trader Richard Dennis. He began this experiment as a result of a bet made with colleague William Eckhardt, and it became wildly successful. Nevertheless, some of the subjects of the experiment were not as profitable as others given the same opportunity. The book also lays out the principles and trading rules of the experiment and offers highly-educational reading for anyone serious about trading.

Further Reading on Technical Analysis and More

Although many other books are available on the subject of stock trading, be sure that your reading on the subject includes a more detailed treatment of technical analysis. This set of techniques that use past price action to forecast the future direction of prices has become an essential subject for any trader to get a grasp of, no matter whether they wish to trade in the stock, forex or commodities markets.

Most seasoned technical analysts would agree that the bible of technical analysis is "Technical Analysis of the Financial Markets: A Comprehensive Guide to Trading Methods and Applications" by John G. Murphy. This book gives a complete overview of all major market and is an invaluable resource for both new and professional traders.

Many other fine books on trading can be found, and the New York Institute of Finance publishes an especially good collection of books on markets and trading. Remember, the more you know about the subject of trading and the market you have chosen to participate in, the more prepared you will be when you make decisions as a trader.

Basically, when it comes to trading, knowledge really is power, and knowing how to apply that knowledge generally distinguishes successful traders from the rest of the pack.

ABOUT THE AUTHORS

Jay and Julie Hawk are a husband and wife team who currently trade financial products online for their own account and have worked in the financial markets in several different occupations. Together, they have more than 40 years of professional experience trading in the financial markets.

For her part, Julie completed her scientific research degree and started out working as a business systems analyst for a major investment bank where she became qualified as a Series 7 Registered Representative and was thoroughly trained in all major financial products. She also attended the well-known O'Connell and Piper options training course in Chicago. She later worked as a dealer in the trading rooms of several major international banks in New York City, London and San Francisco, eventually working her way up to the vice president level.

In that capacity, Julie was personally involved in educating, providing customized hedging and risk taking strategies, meeting with other corporate executives, and handling large scale transactions for high-profile banking clients including large corporations, fund managers and high net worth individuals. She also traded substantial options portfolios for her employers as a risk manager, including exotic options like binary, barrier, average rate and basket options. She even received a notable award for her creativity, teamwork and profitability in executing unusual and highly profitable derivatives transactions.

During that time, Julie also developed world-class expertise in technical analysis, including Elliott Wave Theory, and was involved in initiating research into automated trading and trading signal systems. She also joined the San Francisco Writers' Guild and regularly wrote trade strategies, educational material, market commentary, market newsletters, reports, articles and press releases. In addition, Julie was interviewed for various financial markets magazines and for news wires such as REUTERS in her professional capacity as a financial markets expert.

In contrast to Julie's highly professional and elite banking role, Jay's professional trading experience was focused more on exchange futures and options floor trading activities, fund management, and fundamental research-based stock market investing. After growing up in Chicago and then moving to Mexico City, Jay returned to Chicago to begin working in the financial markets on the Chicago Board Options Exchange just a few years after the exchange was founded.

In addition to working his way up to holding a seat and operating as a market maker on several options exchanges in Chicago and San Francisco, Jay also ran a retail stock brokerage desk and managed funds for a number of large institutional investors that he traded profitably on a discretionary basis. Jay later took a position on the Chicago Mercantile Exchange where he helped start up and actively traded in listed stock index futures and options. He eventually moved to the West Coast to start trading on the Pacific Options Exchange, where he focused on trading stock options and the underlying stocks.

After both independently retiring from their professional trading careers as relatively wealthy people, Jay and Julie met up, fell love and got married to raise a child together just after the new millennium dawned. They moved to Mexico to semi-retire near the beach and operate an Internet-based business together, but they soon discovered that the financial markets had become more accessible to retail traders via online brokers. This incredible opportunity seemed too tempting for these seasoned traders to ignore!

They also observed a demand for educational material to be provided to retail traders via the Internet, and that the quality of existing written content available online was rather poor. That led them to start a new career together as freelance writers specializing in writing about the financial markets using their professional background and expertise. This eventually resulted in them co-founding TheFXperts (located online at www.thefxperts.com) to provide clients with expertly-written financial content, mentoring and financial consulting.

Jay and Julie are very pleased to present this book as the second in a series of books on trading that they will be releasing over the coming years. You can visit TheFXperts' website to learn about their future book releases.

GLOSSARY

Balance Sheet: A financial statement listing a company's assets, liabilities and allocation of shareholder equity at a particular point in time. The balance sheet allows the public to see what the company owns and how much it owes, as well as the stock ownership of the firm.

Capital Markets: Markets where all financial instruments like stocks and bonds, as well as commodities and currencies are traded.

Closing Price: The final closing amount of money at which a security, commodity or other asset has traded at on a given trading day. In markets that trade round the clock, the closing price is determined at a certain hour of the day for the region in which the asset is traded.

Corporation: A legally formed body that is authorized by law to act as a single person regardless of how many people form the body. The corporation is allowed its own rights and duties separate from its members and includes the right of succession.

Dealing Spread: The immediate prices at which a dealer, market maker or specialist is willing to buy and sell a particular stock, commodity or other asset. The dealing spread is composed of a bid, consisting of the highest price a party is willing to pay for an asset; and the offer, the lowest price at which a party is willing to sell a particular asset.

Debt to Equity Ratio: A calculation of a company's liabilities divided by the amount of equity the company has outstanding. The debt to equity ratio is often used to measure the amount of financial leverage of the company and how the company is using its assets in relation to the value of its shareholders' equity.

Discount Broker: A stockbroker that typically fills customer orders for a discounted commission but that does not provide stock market research or investment advice. A full-service stockbroker generally offers their clientele personal consultations, research, and tax and estate planning advice for the higher commissions they charge.

Dividend: A distribution of cash or other asset made by a company to the company's shareholders. The dividend amount or terms is typically decided on by the company's board of directors and the distribution can be made up of cash, shares of stock or other company property.

Earnings per Share: A portion of a company's after-tax earnings allocated to each share of the company's outstanding common stock. Earnings per Share or EPS is an important indicator of a company's profitability and is calculated by taking the company's net income and dividing the amount by the number of outstanding shares. If the company has preferred stock then those dividends are discounted from net income.

Equities: Refers to the ownership interest of a company represented by shares of stock issued by that company. Equities make up the principal source of corporate financing in capitalist economies.

Equity Market: Refers to a system for trading stocks, which represent equity or ownership in the issuing corporations. Stocks are traded in the Equity Market on centralized and non-centralized stock exchanges, as well as over the counter.

Flight to Quality: the tendency of investors to seek the safest possible assets for their money during challenging economic times. By doing so, they generally move their funds out of riskier, low-quality assets and into more conservative, higher-quality assets that are generally perceived as safer investments.

Full Service Broker: A full service broker is a securities dealer that offers their clientele a number of services in addition to filling stock orders on behalf of their clients. Full service brokers generally offer their clients personal consultations, investment advice, research services, and tax and estate planning, as well as other services.

Fundamental Analysis: A method of research that involves determining a stock or other asset's intrinsic value by investigating the related financial and economic factors that influence its valuation. These factors could be related to the company's management, macro or microeconomic data and would determine if the security or asset is fairly valued, undervalued or overvalued.

Initial Public Offering: The first issuance of stock from a private company making the company publicly traded on a stock exchange or over-the-counter network. Initial public offerings are generally made by new companies hoping to raise more capital for expansion; however, large private companies also offer stock to become publicly traded. A company generally has to find an underwriter, which consists of an investment banker that is willing to purchase a percentage of the stock and is responsible for determining the type of security to offer, its valuation and initial distribution. Many initial public offerings have more than one underwriter.

Insider: A senior officer or director of a corporation or any person or entity that holds more than ten percent of a company's voting shares of stock. For the purpose of insider trading, an insider can be anyone who trades shares of a company's stock based on information not readily available to the public. Insiders must comply with disclosure requirements when they make purchases or sales of their equity holdings.

Leverage: In finance, leverage is the use of debt for the financing of an activity. For example, an individual paying for a property with a mortgage or a company that has more than 80 percent debt relative to its assets would be considered leveraged. In stock trading, leverage is achieved by using margin, which calls for a fraction of funds to be deposited in a margin account in order to control the purchase or short sale of securities.

Margin: A collateral amount used in the purchase or short sale of equities. The margin for a stock purchase consists of the collateral amount that the holder of the instrument needs to put up with the counterparty to cover the amount of risk of the transaction. For example, for the purchase of 100 shares of stock, a margin of 20 percent of the total share price is required by the broker or exchange to make the purchase.

Market Capitalization: The value of a company according to the total dollar value of the company's outstanding shares of stock. Also referred to as a company's "market cap", market capitalization is calculated by multiplying the total number of company shares outstanding by the market price of one share of the company's stock. For example, a company with 10 million shares outstanding and their common shares were trading at $10 apiece, would have a market cap of $100 million.

Market Close: The end of a trading session for any particular capital market. For example, the market close of the New York Stock Exchange occurs at the end of trading at 4:00PM Eastern Standard Time and is marked by the ringing of a closing bell. Market close also refers to exchange holidays. In the United States, New Year's Day, Thanksgiving and Christmas are the best known days that markets are closed.

Market Index: A market metric that consists of the weighted values of components included in a particular list of companies. A stock market index shows the performance of a group of component stocks weighted according to their shares outstanding and share price in a mathematical formula, for example the Dow Jones Industrial Average, an index which shows the performance of the 30 top U.S. industrial stocks.

NYSE: An acronym that refers to the New York Stock Exchange. The NYSE is the primary market for the largest capitalization stocks based in the United States and is the world's largest stock exchange in terms of its market capitalization.

Price to Equity Ratio: The ratio of the book value of a common share of a company's stock to the stock's prevailing market price. The book value of an equity is a measure of the shareholder's ownership equity based on the net worth of the company's assets. Therefore, if a stock is trading at $10 per share and the book value of the company is $5 per share, then the Price to Equity ratio would be 2.

Primary Market: The first market where securities are made available through an underwriter. They are traded on the Primary Market before being traded on an exchange or over-the-counter.

Range: The difference between the high and low prices of a stock or other asset during a particular trading time frame. For example, if XYZ stock had a daily high of $11 per share and a daily low of $9 per share, then the Range of that stock during the trading day was $2.

Resistance: A technical term that refers to an excess of supply of an equity or asset at a given price level. For example, if XYZ stock trades up to $12 per share after opening at $10, then the resistance level for that particular time frame would be at $12 per share.

Risk Aversion: A market reaction where an investor is exposed to uncertainty and makes investment decisions that tend to mitigate that uncertainty. For example, a risk averse investor might prefer to buy low-yielding U.S. Treasury Notes instead of taking more risk and purchasing a stock that might have a higher expected returns.

Secondary Market: The market in which securities are freely traded by all market participants. Examples of a Secondary Market include the stock and bond exchanges, commodities futures exchanges and the foreign exchange market.

Securities: Investment instruments of any kind, some of which represent ownership in corporations like stocks, and that are generally traded on secondary markets. Securities include: stocks and bonds, futures contracts, mutual funds and options.

Share Market: The stock or equity market which consists of a system for trading stocks. Stocks represent equity or ownership in the issuing corporations. Stocks are traded on centralized and non-centralized stock exchanges around the world that form the global Share Market.

Share: A single unit of stock ownership in a company. In generally, one Share of stock represents a proportional claim on a company's ownership, its assets and its profits relative to the total amount of shares issued by that company.

Specialist: An exchange member that performs as a market maker and keeps the books on certain exchange traded stocks. For example, a specialist receives all orders of the particular stock they are assigned and posts the bid an offer prices for that stock. In addition, the specialist keeps limit orders on the books and executes at-the-market trades. If the stock goes through a period of low liquidity, the specialist is obligated to make a two sided market in the issue regardless of the level of liquidity.

Stock Dividend: Refers to a dividend paid out to shareholders in shares of stock instead of cash. A Stock Dividend will generally be paid out in proportion to the amount of stock owned by the stockholder. A stock's dividend, on the other hand, is generally paid out to shareholders in cash.

Stock Market: Refers to a system for trading stocks, which represent equity or ownership in their issuing corporations. Stocks are traded on centralized and non-centralized stock exchanges that form a part of the overall Stock Market.

Stock Quote: An indication of the market price for the particular stock that the price is being obtained for. A Stock Quote typically comes with a bid price and an offer price, with the difference known as the spread.

Stock Symbol: The acronym assigned to a company's stock under which their stock is traded on an exchange. Symbols for New York and American Stock Exchange stocks consist of three letters, while stocks listed on the Nasdaq market have four letters.

Stock: Refers to the shares of a corporation which represent an ownership interest in that corporation. Stocks can be issued privately or can be offered to the public and traded on an exchange.

Stockbroker: A legally registered representative that executes buy and sell orders for equities on behalf of their clients. A stockbroker can be either a full service broker or a discount broker. Full service brokers provide their customers with advice, research and other amenities, whereas discount brokers provide only brokering services with no extras.

Support: A technical analysis term that refers to an abundance of buy orders at a certain price level in a security or other asset. When the security reaches a level of support, the stock or other asset tends to move higher until reaching a level — resistance — where an excess of supply puts downward pressure on the stock price.

Technical Analysis: A method of investigation into the price patterns of stocks or other financial assets that depends on the levels of supply and demand. Technical analysis indicates at what prices stocks or other assets are most likely to appreciate or decline by using indicators such as oscillators, moving averages and volume figures.

Ticker Symbol: A two, three or four letter acronym that represents the shares of a company on a tape — commonly known as the ticker tape — that shows all transactions in those and other company shares. For example, the ticker symbol for Apple Inc. is APPL, which is traded on the NASDAQ over-the-counter exchange, while IBM is the ticker symbol for International Business Machines, which is traded on the New York Stock Exchange.

Trend: The prevailing direction of share prices. For example, an upward trend would indicate that share prices are gaining, while a downward trend would indicate share prices were falling. Three major trends can be discerned in the stock market, rising, declining and flat.

JAY AND JULIE HAWK

INDEX

Analysis Paralysis, 98
Anger, 107
Animal Farm, 103
Automated Trading, 64
Averaging, 94
Balance Sheet, 135
Bears, 104
Bid/offer, 61, 63, 95
Bulls, 90, 103, 109
Business Plan, 117
Business Risk, 122, 123, 124
Capital Markets, 135
Cash Accounts, 50
CFD Broker, 65
Chart Patterns, 68, 74, 76
Charting Service, 70
Chickens, 104
Closing Price, 135
Commitment of Traders, 84
Consolidation Patterns, 76
Consumer Price Index, 84
Continuation Patterns, 76
Corporation, 135
Day Traders, 56
Day Trading, 55
Dealing Spread, 61, 135
Debt to Equity Ratio, 136

Demo Testing, 118
Depression, 107
Directional Movement Indicator, 72
Discipline, 59, 97, 111, 119
Discount Broker, 44, 136
Discretionary Accounts, 51
Dividend, 136
Double Top or Bottom, 77
Doubling Up, 94
Earnings per Share, 136
Economic Data, 83
Economic Risk, 124
Edwin Lefevre, 129
Emotional Responses, 121
Emotions, 94, 102, 105, 106, 107, 109, 110, 121, 126
Employment Data, 84
Equities, 136
Equity Market, 136
Excitement, 107
Fear, 102, 106, 108
Flags, 76
Flight to Quality, 136
Full Service Broker, 137
Full-Service Brokerage, 50
Fundamental Analysis, 82, 137

Fundamentals, 26, 84, 86
Geopolitical events, 84
Greed, 90, 94, 96, 102, 103, 105, 106, 108, 109, 112, 120
Gross Domestic Product, 84
Head and Shoulders, 77
Hope, 102, 106, 109
Human Behavior, 82
Illiquidity, 95
Industrial Production, 84
Initial Public Offering, 137
Insider, 137
Jack Schwager, 130
John G. Murphy, 130
Leverage, 137
Limit Orders, 36
Managing Emotions, 109
Margin, 138
Margin Accounts, 50
Margin Calls, 58, 110, 124
Market Capitalization, 138
Market Close, 138
Market Index, 138
Market Orders, 35
Market-Makers, 61
Market-Making, 61
MetaTrader, 64, 65, 71, 80
Michael Covel, 130
Mindset, 111, 114
Money Management, 40, 89, 91, 92, 118
Moving Averages, 63, 72, 75
News, 81, 87
NYSE, 138
OCO Order. *See* One-Cancels-the-Other Order
One-Cancels-the-Other Order, 37
Online Broker, 26
Online Stock Broker, 46, 65
Online Stock Trading, 46
Over Leveraging, 94
Overtrading, 98, 108

Pattern-Matching, 78
Pennants, 77
Pigs, 105
Position Sizing, 91, 114
Price Analysis, 67
Price to Equity Ratio, 138
Primary Market, 139
Probability of Success, 40
Producer Price Index, 84
Psychology, 101, 102, 110, 118
Range, 139
Range Traders, 58
Rectangles, 77
Relative Strength Index, 60, 69, 72, 75
Resistance, 69, 75, 139
Retail Sales, 84
Reversal Patterns, 77
Risk Aversion, 139
Risk Management, 92, 120
Risks, 95, 109, 123, 124, 127
RSI. *See* Relative Strength Index
Scalping, 61
Secondary Market, 139
Securities, 139
Share, 139
Share Market, 139
Sheep, 104
Specialist, 140
Stock, 1, 25, 37, 38, 39, 55, 59, 63, 67, 73, 85, 86, 95, 96, 97, 103, 117, 121, 122, 123, 126, 140
Stock Broker, 45, 51
Stock Brokerage, 45
Stock Dividend:, 140
Stock Market, 140
Stock Options, 38
Stock Quote, 140
Stock Symbol, 140
Stock Trading Robots, 65
Stock Valuation, 85
Stockbroker, 26, 35, 43, 49, 140

Stocks, 26
Stop Orders, 36
Stop-loss Orders, 91
Supply and demand, 84
Support, 69, 75, 141
Swing Trading, 59, 60
Taking Profits, 108
Tax Code, 124
Technical Analysis, 26, 67, 69, 70, 78, 80, 86, 130, 141
Technical Analysis Software, 78, 79, 80
Technical Indicators, 69, 72, 73, 74
Technical Newsletter, 69
Ticker Symbol, 141
Trade Balance, 84
Trade Journal, 112
Trade Plan, 71, 119, 120, 121, 122, 127
Trade Signal Generating Software, 79
Trader Psychology, 101
Trading, 91
Trading Decisions, 126

Trading Goals, 118
Trading Mechanics, 25
Trading Mentor, 126
Trading Pitfalls, 126
Trading Plan, 27, 40, 56, 59, 71, 75, 89, 91, 92, 93, 96, 101, 108, 109, 111, 112, 113, 114, 118, 119, 120, 122
Trading Psychology, 118
Trading Risks, 95, 96, 97, 98
Trading Robot, 64, 65, 79
Trading Signals, 73
Trading Software, 63, 79
Trading Strategies, 55
Trading Tips, 39, 125
Trailing Stops, 92
Trend, 141
Trend Traders, 57
Trend Trading, 57, 60
Triangles, 76, 77
Triple Top or Bottom, 77
Volatility, 95
Volume Indicators, 73
Wedges, 77

www.ingramcontent.com/pod-product-compliance
Lightning Source LLC
Chambersburg PA
CBHW020424220526
45464CB00002B/564